MUTINY ON THE BOUNTY

NOTES

including

- *About the Authors*
- *List of Characters*
- *Genealogies*
- *Brief Plot Synopsis*
- *Illustration: The* Bounty *and Its Rigging*
- *Summaries & Critical Commentaries*
- *Critical Essays*
    Mutiny on the Bounty: The Historical Background
    The Historical William Bligh
    Movies Based on the Mutiny on the *Bounty*
- *Suggested Essay Questions*
- *Selected Bibliography*

by
Gregory Tubach
University of Nebraska

INCORPORATED

LINCOLN, NEBRASKA 68501

Editor

Gary Carey, M.A.
University of Colorado

Consulting Editor

James L. Roberts, Ph.D.
Department of English
University of Nebraska

ISBN 0-8220-0860-2
© Copyright 1990
by
C. K. Hillegass
All Rights Reserved
Printed in U.S.A.

1992 Printing

Jacksonville Public Libraries (FL)

Cliffs Notes, Inc.   Lincoln, Nebraska

CONTENTS

MUTINY ON THE BOUNTY

Notes

ABOUT THE AUTHORS

Charles Nordhoff and James Hall were both published authors when they first met at the end of World War I. Both men had distinguished themselves as flyers in the famed Lafayette Escadrille Corps, and while serving in the squadron, each of them wrote articles for the *Atlantic Monthly* about their wartime experiences. When the war ended, the two men were asked to write a book about the history of the Escadrille, and this collaboration was the beginning of a long and successful venture for the two.

Nordhoff suggested to Hall that they should move to the Tahitian Islands to write about the South Sea. The men approached the *Atlantic Monthly's* editor about the idea and were advanced $7000 for their expenses. Their first collaboration about the South Sea, *Faery Lands*, sold fairly well, but the collaboration deteriorated, and the two men began writing on their own again.

Nordhoff concentrated his efforts on writing books for boys, publishing *Pearl Lagoon* shortly after his split with Hall. Hall did not fare as well. He struggled to sell short articles about the lives of the island people and became increasingly morose. Tired of island life, Hall approached a publisher about writing a travel book on Iceland. He was given a $5000 advance and travelled to Iceland, where he did his research and finished the book. It was a dismal failure, so Hall decided to return to Tahiti. His return to the island marked a new beginning.

During this time, Nordhoff continued to try his hand at boys books and attained a respectable name for himself. In the span of four years, he published three adventure books, married a Tahitian woman, and fathered several children. Strong drink and growing depression, however, caused Nordhoff to begin to question his ability as a writer. When Hall returned from Iceland, the two men decided again to try to collaborate on a novel.

This conjunction marked the turning point in their literary careers. With Hall tempering Nordhoff's uncontrollable energy and Nordhoff inspiring Hall's imagination, the two embarked on a sea of best sellers, including *Falcons of France: A Tale of Youth and the Air* (1929), *The Hurricane* (1936), *Dark River* (1938), *No More Gas* (1940), *Botany Bay* (1941), *Men Without Country* (1942), and *The High Barbaree* (1945). The pinnacle of their success, however, was published between *Falcons of France* and *The Hurricane:* the *Mutiny* trilogy: *Mutiny on the Bounty* (1932), in which the *Bounty* is seized from Captain Bligh by Fletcher Christian, who then sails out in search of an uninhabited island; *Men Against the Sea* (1934), which recounts Bligh's open-boat voyage to England to report the mutiny; and *Pitcairn's Island* (1934), which tells about Christian's finding Pitcairn Island and how the lives of the mutineers changed during their stay on the island.

Nordhoff and Hall gained critical acclaim for their trilogy, and especially for *Mutiny on the Bounty*, which was a Book-of-the-Month Club selection. After the success of this trilogy, Nordhoff became disillusioned with writing, yet he continued to collaborate with Hall, turning out several more popular novels. With the completion of *The High Barbaree*, however, there was little doubt in either author's mind that this one would be the last book written together by the two men. Nordhoff wanted to return to Tahiti, but he went instead to his parents' home during a fierce bout of depression, and he died there on April 11, 1947, a broken man yearning for his paradise of Tahiti.

Hall's success continued after *The High Barbaree*. He returned to his hometown in Iowa, and there, he worked on more novels and short essays. Writing alone once again, his work was now received far better. His later works include *A Word for His Sponsor: A Narrative Poem* (1949) and *The Far Lands* (1950), which was a Literary Guild selection.

In 1951, knowing that he was dying, Hall and his wife returned to Tahiti, where his condition deteriorated quickly. He died on July 6 and was buried with Tahitian funeral rites. Afterward, three of his works were published posthumously: *The Forgotten One, and Other*

True Tales of the South Seas (1952), *Her Daddy's Best Ice Cream* (1952), and *My Island Home* (1952).

LIST OF CHARACTERS

Roger Byam

The fictitious narrative character used by the authors to tell the story of the mutiny on the *Bounty*. Historically, there was no such person as Byam; he is simply a creation of the authors in order to dramatize the latter portion of the novel. At the beginning of the novel, Roger is seventeen years old. He attracts the attention of Captain Bligh because of his unique ability to learn quickly and master the intricacies of foreign languages. Because the sailors of the South Sea need to learn the language prevalent in that part of the world in order to trade with the natives, the British government hires Byam to compile a dictionary of the Tahitian language and an accompanying grammar book. Early in the novel, we discover that Byam comes from a highly respected family and that he is a man of absolute integrity.

Captain William Bligh

The captain of the *Bounty*, he is sailing to Tahiti to gather bread-fruit trees, whose fruit will be used as cheap food for the slaves of the British landowners in the West Indies. Bligh's strict disciplinary measures will be directly responsible for the seizure of the *Bounty* by Lieutenant Fletcher Christian and his followers. Bligh's unreasonable behavior, coupled with the crew's knowledge that he has been cheating them of their due rations, makes most of them despise him. Bligh's harsh punishments for minor offenses (or, often, imagined acts) make him an object of scorn and eventually cause the men to mutiny against him. Bligh, however, is an immensely skilled navigator, and he leads his small band of survivors over a great expanse of sea to safety—seemingly, an almost impossible feat.

Fletcher Christian

One of the ranking officers on the *Bounty*, Christian comes from genteel stock and finally finds it impossible to endure all of the insults heaped upon him by Captain Bligh. His statement that most men can be ruled by kindness and reason is ridiculed by Bligh, and when Christian is accused of theft and alleged conspiracy, he leads the others in a mutiny. Subsequently, he is declared captain of the *Bounty* and the leader of a band of mutineers, whom he ultimately guides to an unknown island. Throughout the novel, Christian is depicted as an honest man, one who has never done anything dishonorable. In fact, it is his strong sense of honesty which makes him burn with shame when he is accused of something dishonest; in addition, his shame is made even more intolerable because he is humiliated in front of the crew. The movies made from this novel usually depict Christian in heroic proportions.

Chapter 10 focuses almost wholly on Christian's character, emphasizing his deep sense of the wrong that he feels he suffers at the hands of Captain Bligh. Byam understands and empathizes with Fletcher Christian's feelings, but once the mutiny occurs, Byam does not sympathize with Christian's plight.

John Fryer

Master of the *Bounty*. In spite of the fact that he strongly dislikes Captain Bligh, he is nevertheless loyal to the King's Navy, and he is the type of man whom Fletcher Christian will *not* want to have on board the *Bounty* after the mutiny because Christian knows that despite the fact that Fryer detests Bligh, Fryer will make every effort to retake the *Bounty*. His testimony at Byam's court-martial should clear the young man, but unfortunately it doesn't.

Robert Tinkler

Tinkler is Mr. Fryer's brother-in-law. We first encounter him as a victim of Bligh's infamous and unjust punishments: the young man is forced to undergo severe hardships for being awake after all candles were to be extinguished and the men in their berths. While he is not Byam's closest friend, they are good comrades. Tinkler's key scene in the novel occurs as he overhears a conversation between Byam and Christian, when Byam tells Christian, "You can count on me, sir." Tinkler's main function lies in his being "resurrected" so that he can repeat the whole of this conversation to the Royal High Admiralty, testimony which will acquit Roger Byam.

Thomas Hayward and John Hallet

These two men are the midshipmen who could testify in Byam's behalf; instead, they want to cover up the fact that both of them cried and whimpered to stay aboard the *Bounty* after Christian had taken command of the ship. Villainously, they implicate both James Morrison and Roger Byam in the mutiny. Hallet, in particular, has a grudge against Morrison and Byam because they caught him informing on his comrades, and they witnessed his disgraceful bawling during the conclusion of the mutiny.

Thomas Huggan

The surgeon aboard the *Bounty*, the ship's "saw-bones." Huggan drinks a lot and prescribes alcohol as a remedy for every ailment that befalls the crew. For example, after Tinkler is taken down from the bone-chilling mast after twenty-four hours, Huggan gives him a strong shot of rum, which allows Tinkler to return to service on deck, "none the worse for his night aloft."

When the good-natured surgeon dies on Tahiti, men such as Fletcher Christian know that he will be sorely missed because of his good humor and his humane treatment of the sailors.

David Nelson

The botanist who knows of Byam's loyalty and who could have testified about Byam's wish to join Bligh in the launch. His untimely death removes a key witness for Byam.

John Norton

The quartermaster who could have corroborated Christian's intention to escape from the *Bounty* on a raft built by Norton during the night preceding the mutiny. His death is particularly untimely since the members of the court-martial board think that it is unbelievable that a quartermaster would be doing carpenter work when there were two qualified carpenters on the ship. The court-martial board does not believe Byam's testimony about Norton building a raft for Christian because they feel Byam *chose* to say this about Norton because he knew Norton to be dead and unable to substantiate Byam's testimony.

William Purcell

The unpleasant carpenter, whose tyranny is surpassed only by the tyranny of Captain Bligh. The two men — captain and carpenter — despise one another, but as much as Purcell hates Bligh, he is loyal to Bligh and will have absolutely nothing to do with the mutineers, whom he calls scoundrels and outlaws.

Mr. Samuel

The clerk who helps Captain Bligh cheat the men out of their fair share of rations. Next to Bligh and Purcell, he is the most detested person aboard the *Bounty*.

James Morrison

The boatswain's mate, Morrison joins Byam and Stewart in secretly planning to retake the *Bounty* after Christian has bound Bligh, but their plans are foiled when their guard is doubled. Morrison is unable to join Bligh in the launch because of the crowded conditions in the small boat; therefore, he is forced to remain on board the ship, along with Byam. As a result of this act of fate, he is found guilty of mutiny, but because of extenuating circumstances aboard the *Bounty*, the court-martial board grants Morrison clemency.

Thomas Ellison

The youthful boy who has nothing to do with the mutiny, yet once it begins, he delights in taunting Bligh. He has undergone much suffering at the hands of the tyrannical and irrational Captain Bligh, and it is understandable that he would want to offer one last taunt at Bligh. For this adolescent indiscretion, he is hanged.

Captain Edwards

The captain of the *Pandora*, whose mission is to search out, find, and return to England all of the *Bounty*'s mutineers for trial. Edwards carries out "the letter of the law" with no concept of the "spirit of the law." At times, he seems to be brutal, hateful, spiteful, despicable, obnoxious, and as cruel as Bligh himself.

Lieutenant Parkin

Captain Edwards' lieutenant aboard the *Pandora*; he delights in sadistically and unnecessarily punishing the prisoners. For example, while the ship is anchored in the harbor of Tahiti, amidst a plethora of fresh meat and fresh fruit, he sadistically forces the prisoners to eat moldy, hard-tack biscuits and dry meat.

Captain Montague

The captain of the *H.M.S. Hector*, on which the accused mutineers are imprisoned. In contrast to the other captains whom we have seen in this novel, Captain Montague is humane, decent, and very considerate of their mental and physical welfare. For example, Captain Montague treats Byam as a gentleman, allowing Byam to read his letters in private, as well as take exercises in the open; in general, he treats Byam with the humanity due Byam. After Byam is cleared of the charge of mutiny, Montague asks Byam to join him in Montague's next excursion at sea.

Dr. Hamilton

As the doctor aboard the *Pandora*, he continually intercedes for the benefit of the prisoners; he sees that their quarters are clean and that they are well fed, and he uses his influence with Captain Edwards to secure some small amenities for them. He remains firm in his belief that Byam is innocent of mutiny, and he continues to support Byam even after Byam is convicted and sentenced to death.

Sir Joseph Banks

Byam's influential friend who is responsible for Byam's first meeting with Bligh; later, he is Byam's staunchest defender during the court-martial. To Byam, Sir Joseph is one of those exceptional men who seem to be a member of a race apart from all others, the type of man who finds himself equally at home among common seamen or among the lords of the realm. In appearance, he is described as being a typical Englishman, one who could have been taken from a Dickens novel. He is solidly built, yet seems to radiate energy and strength, and is one of the busiest and most influential men in London. Part of Sir Joseph's influence comes from his being president of the prestigious Royal Society, an organization which has influence in all spheres of English life.

Officially, Sir Joseph is anxious for Byam to undertake a journey on the *Bounty* in order to complete a dictionary of the Tahitian language for use in Britain's vast trading and colonization network. Throughout the trial, and afterwards, Sir Joseph remains convinced of Byam's innocence, and when Byam is condemned to die, Sir Joseph announces that no greater injustice has ever been perpetrated than that against Byam: "There has never been a more tragic miscarriage of justice in the history of His Majesty's Navy." The fact that Sir Joseph uses his influence as president of the Royal Society to gain Byam an extra month to finish his dictionary also gives him enough time to find Tinkler and submit his testimony on Byam's behalf. At the end of the novel, Sir Joseph is influential in convincing Byam to make the navy his vocation.

Mr. Graham

The naval officer who acts as Byam's advocate during the court-martial proceedings. As a naval officer, Mr. Graham is cautious, yet totally convinced of Byam's innocence.

Mr. Erskine

Byam's father's attorney and a friend of the family. After the court-martial, he provides Byam with a quiet sanctuary so that Byam can put the horrible tribulations he has undergone into perspective.

Hitihiti

The Tahitian chief who befriends Byam and helps him formulate the Tahitian dictionary. Byam lives with Hitihiti and becomes part of his household until Byam marries the beautiful Tehani.

Tehani

The exquisitely lovely Tahitian princess who becomes Byam's wife and, later, the mother of their daughter, Helen. When Byam is imprisoned aboard the *Pandora*, Tehani wants to lead a revolt against the ship in an attempt to free Byam, but Byam convinces her that to attempt to free him would lead to the annihilation of vast numbers of Tahitians.

Roger Byam's Genealogy

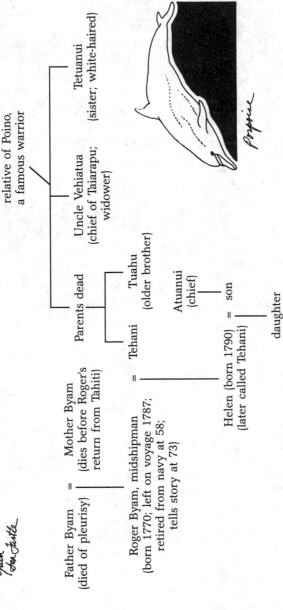

relative of Poino, a famous warrior

Parents dead

Uncle Vehiatua (chief of Taiarapu; widower)

Tetuanui (sister; white-haired)

Tuahu (older brother)

Tehani

Atuanui (chief)

Father Byam = Mother Byam (dies before Roger's return from Tahiti)

Roger Byam, midshipman (born 1770; left on voyage 1787; retired from navy at 58; tells story at 73)

Helen (born 1790) (later called Tehani) =

son

daughter

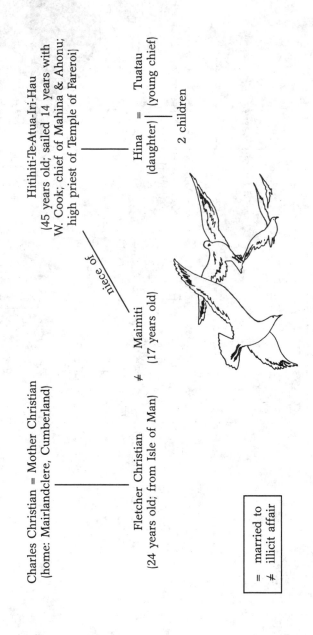

Fletcher Christian's Genealogy

Hitihiti-Te-Atua-Iri-Hau
(45 years old; sailed 14 years with
W. Cook; chief of Mahina & Ahonu;
high priest of Temple of Fareroi)

niece of

Maimiti
(17 years old)

Charles Christian = Mother Christian
(home: Mairlandclere, Cumberland)

Fletcher Christian   ≠   Maimiti
(24 years old; from Isle of Man)

Hina   =   Tuatau
(daughter) (young chief)

2 children

= married to
≠ illicit affair

BRIEF PLOT SYNOPSIS

Roger Byam is introduced to the reader, and we learn that he has been extended an invitation by Captain William Bligh to embark on an expedition to Tahiti to gather breadfruit trees and take them to the West Indies, where they will be planted and their fruit fed to the slaves of English colonists. Byam is expected to formulate a dictionary of the Tahitian language.

The *Bounty* sets sail in November, 1787, and its crew is introduced to the reader. The ship makes calls on several islands during its journey to Tahiti, and, meanwhile, conditions aboard the ship begin to deteriorate. Food rots, the crew suspects Bligh of hoarding food for himself, and several men are accused of stealing. Discontent is mounting among the crew.

The *Bounty* reaches Tahiti, and Byam begins studying the Tahitian language with the aid of some of the natives. Members of the crew begin the task of digging up young breadfruit trees and storing them on board the ship. Many of the men form attachments to the Tahitian women, and the realization that the *Bounty* will soon be sailing from this idyllic life causes grumbling among the crew. Not surprisingly, three men desert before the ship leaves.

The *Bounty* sets sail for the West Indies to deliver the trees, and early in the voyage, Bligh harasses his crew — in particular, he accuses some of them of stealing coconuts. His officers, notably Fletcher Christian, begin grumbling over the poor treatment that they are receiving at the hands of Bligh. Accordingly, one morning, some of the crew, led by Christian, seize the ship and force Bligh, along with some of Bligh's followers, into the *Bounty's* launch to fend for themselves on the high seas. Those who wish to accompany Bligh but cannot because of the already-crowded conditions in the launch are forced to remain with the mutineers aboard the *Bounty*.

Christian immediately begins sailing the South Sea in search of an uninhabited island, but finding none and tired of the complaints of his fellow mutineers, Christian returns to Tahiti, where he drops off those who wish to stay on the island, including Byam. Then he resumes his search for an unchartered and uninhabited island.

Byam eases himself back into the idyllic life he experienced the first time on the island, and soon he marries a Tahitian princess. A child is born to the couple, and life on Tahiti continues to be a paradise—until an English ship drops anchor at the island. Byam rows out to meet the vessel and is immediately imprisoned as a mutineer, along with the other Englishmen on the island.

While taking the prisoners back to England to be tried for mutiny, the ship runs aground on a reef and sinks, but not before the crew and prisoners have taken refuge in the ship's smaller boats. The small boats make an open-sea journey, and finally, after several months of sailing and torturous conditions, they reach land safely. The mutineers are imprisoned aboard another vessel, which takes them back to England to await their court-martial.

The court-martial of Byam and his companions begins. Testimony is given by the men of the *Bounty* who made it back to England. Byam and the other men are then allowed to present their defenses. The judges deliberate and find Byam, along with five of the other nine men, guilty of mutiny against the *Bounty*.

Three of the six condemned men are taken to be hanged, and the other three, Byam included, are spared the rope only hours before their seemingly inevitable deaths. Byam is spared because Robert Tinkler, a friend of Byam's aboard the *Bounty*, corroborates Byam's testimony at the court-martial concerning his innocence, and the other two men are saved from hanging after being pardoned by the proper British authorities.

Byam returns to his family home to live out his life, but is persuaded into duty aboard another ship by the ship's captain. The ship battles the Dutch off the coast of Spain and is victorious.

Byam is promoted to captain, given his own ship, and ordered to sail to the South Sea. While there, he sets anchor at Tahiti, where he learns that his wife is dead, but that their daughter is alive. He meets with Helen, now grown, but does not reveal his identity to her. The novel closes with Byam reviewing the events of his past and contemplating the future.

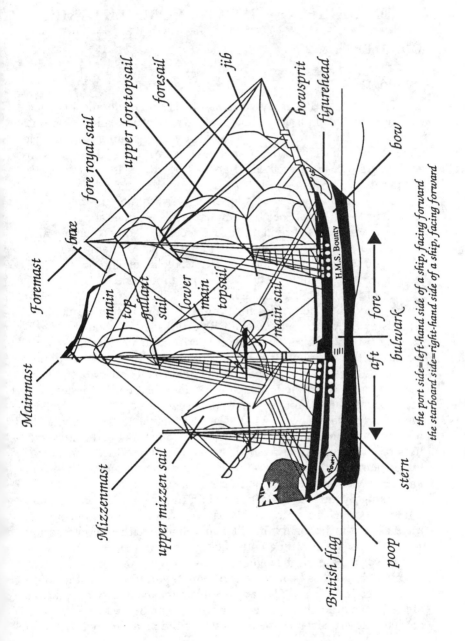

Mairmast

Foremast

Mizzenmast

upper mizzen sail

British flag

Mainmast

brace

fore royal sail

upper foretopsail

foresail

jib

bowsprit

figurehead

bow

main top gallant sail

lower main topsail

main sail

H.M.S. Bounty

aft ← fore →

bulwark

poop

stern

the port side=left-hand side of a ship, facing forward
the starboard side=right-hand side of a ship, facing forward

SUMMARIES & CRITICAL COMMENTARIES

CHAPTERS 1 & 2

Summary

The narrator, Roger Byam, tells of his home life and his background. He lives in a very conservative part of England, where his highly respected family has resided for over five hundred years. He then takes us back into the past. The year is 1787, and he is seventeen years old and expected to go to Oxford, as is the custom in his family.

One morning, however, a letter arrives from Sir Joseph Banks, president of the Royal Society, famous for his writings about explorations. He was a close friend of Roger's recently deceased father, and, in his letter, he tells them that a certain Captain William Bligh, who was an officer with the famous Captain Cook, an explorer of the Tahitian Islands, is visiting friends in the neighborhood.

Accordingly, the Byams extend Captain Bligh an invitation to their home, and when he arrives for dinner, the discussion turns to the islands of the South Sea. Captain Bligh tells them about his forthcoming trip to Tahiti in order to collect breadfruit trees as a cheap staple for the slaves of British gentry stationed in the West Indies. He has also been commissioned to formulate a dictionary of the Tahitian language, which he is incapable of doing. However, on learning that Roger has a gift for languages (he speaks fluent French, Italian, Latin, and is mastering German), Captain Bligh extends an invitation for Roger to join the expedition in order to compile a Tahitian dictionary. Surprisingly, since she is a recent widow, Roger's mother is wholeheartedly for the project, even though it will mean a two-year journey away from home for Roger.

Young Byam goes to London to join the crew of the *Bounty*, and while there, he visits Sir Joseph Banks, who gives him encouragement about the dictionary; it will be invaluable to the merchants and seamen who are traveling and trading in that area.

Toward the end of November, Byam joins the *Bounty*, whose "great cabin aft" has been converted into a garden for the reception of the breadfruit trees. This arrangement makes the living quarters of the men extremely cramped: four men to an 8 × 10 foot area; each of them has virtually no space to move around in, and only one person can get out of his berth at a time. Byam is then introduced to the first mate, Fletcher Christian, "a fine figure of a seaman," the master, Mr. Fryer, and the surgeon, Thomas Huggan.

Bligh and Byam are then invited to board another ship, the *Tigress*, to have dinner with the captain, and while they are on board, they witness the flogging of an able-bodied seaman who has died—yet continues to receive an additional 24 lashes with the cat-of-nine-tails. After this episode, the three go to the captain's cabin. Bligh and the host captain eat as though nothing happened. Byam, however, has little appetite.

Commentary

The opening of the novel functions as a prologue to the entire novel. We first learn that the narrator of the novel has spent some forty years of his life at sea and now, at seventy-three, retired, and with much time on his hands, has decided to write about his adventures on the high seas. Of all his adventures at sea, he singles out the most significant: the mutiny aboard the *Bounty*. As a result of that mutiny, he was locked in irons, brought back to England, tried by a court-martial, and condemned to die by hanging. The prologue therefore arouses our curiosity because we are obviously interested in learning how he escaped death.

While this novel is based upon a historically true incident, the authors use their poetic license—that is, they change reality to create a fictional narrator, "Roger Byam," who will tell the story. They choose "Byam" in order to make the narrative more interesting: he will be representing the viewpoint of the upper class, a young man who is very conservative, a characteristic not readily associated with the concept of mutiny. He will be an innocent man, caught up in a tangled web of good and evil.

Sir Joseph Banks, who will become Byam's strongest defender at the end of the book, when Roger is accused of treason, is also introduced to the reader. Sir Joseph functions as the intermediary in introducing Byam to Captain William Bligh, who was with Captain Cook on his famous expeditions to the South Sea. At this time, the adventures of Captain Cook were well-known throughout Europe; his investigations into little-known cultures led many people to read the writings of Jean Jacques Rousseau, who wrote extensively upon the "natural life of the native Indian," uncorrupted by modern civilization.

This idea is often referred to as the Noble Savage concept. It is an idealistic and romantic belief which Captain Bligh doesn't accept; in contrast to Rousseau, who believed in the nobility of the savage, Bligh is a realist who has no illusions about the natives. He knows that they are superstitious and live in a rigid, hierarchical society.

Chapter 1 also provides us with the reason for Byam's being taken on the expedition: his expert grasp of foreign languages makes him the perfect choice to formulate a dictionary of the Tahitian language. According to Sir Joseph, the value of such a dictionary is inestimable because the language is spoken over a great portion of the South Sea area and will be of great benefit for commerce with the islanders.

At the end of Chapter 1, we learn from Sir Joseph that Captain Bligh has a reputation for being a hard taskmaster and that he is infamous for his belief in "discipline's the thing." This knowledge foreshadows the later mutiny since Captain Bligh's indiscriminate and harsh application of unreasonable discipline will be one of the causes of the mutiny.

Another cause of the mutiny is introduced in Chapter 2. The ship, which is small, is cramped even further when the captain turns the great cabin into a garden, forcing the men to live in an area that is incredibly small. One should always keep in mind that the mutiny is not caused by one single incident. The novel presents multiple reasons for the seizure of the ship.

The incident of the dead man being flogged emphasizes the severity of "sea law" – law so severe that it will later be directly related to the mutiny. The incident is so unnerving to young Byam that he loses his appetite, and yet the incident has no effect at all on the experienced captains, who, as we learn later, have extensive experience in meting out severe punishment.

In addition to the above event, this chapter emphasizes the severity, and the need, of "sea law." As we see later, this sea law allows the captain to be an absolute tyrant because the seamen have no recourse for redress.

(Here and in the following chapters, difficult words and phrases, as well as slang, nautical terms, and the like are translated, as are those below.)

- **aft**   toward the stern, or tail, of the boat.

- **midshipman** a sub-lieutenant, a young cadet.

- **blotted log** a water-spotted ship's journal.

- **in irons** having wide, iron cuffs around the wrists and ankles.

- **Captain Cook** an English navigator and explorer (1728–79). Rediscovered the Hawaiian Islands (Sandwich Islands). Killed by Hawaiian natives.

- **woolgathering** dreamy, inattentive.

- **petitioned the Crown** petitioned the king and/or Parliament.

- **breadfruit** melon-shaped fruit on medium-sized trees native to the tropics; the pulp resembles fresh bread.

- **the cut of his jib** his personal appearance.

- **the old tars** old sailors.

- **our solicitor** our lawyer.

- **the Royal Society** an organization founded in 1662 to advance scientific knowledge, particularly the physical sciences, and further research.

- **cockades** rosettes or knots of ribbon, usually worn on a hat, indicating rank.

- **forced to mess with** forced to eat with.

- **wherries** light, shallow rowboats.

- **bumboat men** men who provide a ship with fresh provisions.

- **the master's mate** an officer who is subordinate to the master.

- **your berth** your bed, or sleeping place.

- **the larboard side** starboard side; the right-hand side of a ship when looking forward.

- **a quadrant** a navagational instrument used for measuring altitudes.

- **bilge water** water that seeps into a boat and sours.

- **of gentle birth** well-born; born to honorable, upper-class parents.

- **a man-of-war** an armed naval ship.

- **sup** eat with.

- **the new reefers** slang for new midshipmen.

- **our sawbones** our surgeon, or doctor.

- **halliards** halyards; ropes or tackle for raising or lowering a sail.

- **the boatswain** the ship's officer in charge of sails and rigging and summoning men to duty.

- **a quizzing glass** a monocle, or single eyeglass.

- **his powdered queue** a powdered pigtail.

- **keel-hauling** hauling a person under the keel (the lowest part of a ship) for punishment.

CHAPTERS 3 & 4

Summary

After a month's delay due to bad weather, the *Bounty* sets out to sea on the twenty-third of December. During that time, young Byam is taught trigonometry, nautical astrology, and navigation, along with two of his fellow midshipmen: George Stewart, a seaman who has made other voyages before his current stint on the *Bounty*, and Edward Young. Others on board are also introduced to the reader: Mr. Nelson, the botanist, who will care for the young breadfruit trees; Hallet, a sickly looking boy of fifteen; Tinkler, fourteen years old and a good friend of Byam's throughout the voyage; and Hayward, one of Byam's berth-mates. Hayward feels superior to Byam because this is Byam's first voyage at sea and Hayward's second. Thomas Ellison is the mess boy for Byam and his berth-mates.

Food and drink are abundant at the beginning of the voyage, with each man receiving a gallon of beer daily, but during a heavy storm, many casks are lost, and the men must be content with wine. Also damaged during the storm is a large portion of the bread, which was stored below deck.

The island of Teneriffe is sighted on the fourth of January, and for five days, the *Bounty* lies anchored there. Captain Bligh refuses shore leave for the men and also stops the allowance of salt beef. Instead, he substitutes very low-grade fresh beef obtained from the island. Both of these actions cause grumbling among the men. They say that they would rather eat nothing at all than the "fresh beef" which they suspect is cut from the carcasses of dead horses. As a result, most of the meat is thrown overboard.

After setting sail from Teneriffe, Bligh divides the men into three watches, putting Fletcher Christian in charge of the third watch. (This fact will be of importance later on in the novel when Bligh remembers seeing Christian and Byam talking secretly; Bligh will imagine that they are plotting mutiny.) As head of the third watch, Christian becomes a lieutenant and second-in-command of the ship, much to the dissatisfaction of his former superior, Master Fryer, who now must take orders from Christian.

Bligh informs the men that because of the uncertainty of the length of the voyage, the allowance of bread will be cut by one-third. The food given the men during the *Bounty*'s voyage is handed out by Mr. Samuel, Bligh's clerk, who regularly keeps back a portion which is due for the men for himself and Bligh. The men are not ignorant of this cheating; they know that they are being robbed of what is rightfully theirs and, as a result, there is more grumbling among them.

Being a captain who knows every detail of his ship, Bligh announces that fifty pounds of cheese is missing, and he accuses the men of having stolen it. Hillbrandt, the cooper, reminds Bligh that he himself ordered the cheese to be taken ashore to Bligh's house before the *Bounty* left port. Bligh calls him an "insolent scoundrel" and demands that Mr. Samuel stop the men's allowance of cheese—and the officers' allowance, as well. Everyone, especially the officers, are taken aback by this order.

Very soon into the voyage, the provisions obtained before the *Bounty* set sail begin to dwindle. The remaining bread is infested with maggots and the small amount of salt beef aboard is so hard that Alexander Smith, one of the able seaman, carves a snuffbox for the surgeon out of it. The dissatisfaction of the men—and the officers—continues to grow.

Bligh invites Byam to dine with him, along with Fryer and Christian, his usual guests. The conversation turns to the flogging of Thomas Burkitt, on the preceding day. Bligh stresses the need for severity when dealing with the men, while Christian offers the suggestion that a little kindness might do just as well. Christian's suggestion is scoffed at by Bligh, who damns all the men aboard the *Bounty*. Byam perceives that Fryer dislikes the captain because of the cheese incident and that Christian, too, has contempt for the captain. The meal is anything but congenial.

Following Bligh's orders, Samuel begins to distribute pumpkins, which were obtained on the island of Teneriffe, in place of bread. The men feel that this is unfair, and Bligh, hearing of the men's discontent, threatens them, shouting, "I'll make you eat grass before I've done with you!" The men cease their grumbling, but the officers continue to talk among themselves about their continual state of hunger. Meanwhile, Bligh and his clerk continue to pilfer the ship's rations.

The *Bounty* reaches the coast of Brazil and stands becalmed due to the wind. The men spend their time wishing for a way to supplement their scant rations. John Mills, the gunner's mate, catches a shark and is rationing it between the men when Samuel tells Mills that a piece of the shark must be provided for the captain's table. Mills throws a chunk at Samuel, hitting him in the face, and leaves the deck. As a result, Mills is ordered by Bligh to spend the night in irons and is flogged with 36 lashes the following day.

Captain Bligh decides to steer for the Cape of Good Hope. Fine weather helps the spirits of the men on board, and they begin to play pranks on each other. But their fun and games is quelled when Tinkler, playing a card game late at night (when all the men are supposed to be in their bunks) gets caught by Bligh and is sent to the top of the main masthead.

Fearful that Tinkler is dying aloft, Christian climbs the mast in the morning and helps Tinkler down to the deck. Blue and stiff with cold, Tinkler is taken to the surgeon, who gives him spoonfuls of rum to revive him.

On the twenty-third of May, the *Bounty* drops anchor near Cape Town and stays there for a month before continuing its voyage, reaching Adventure Bay on the twentieth of August, when they stop for water and saw planks from the local timber.

Purcell, the carpenter, is instructed by Bligh to fell large eucalyptus trees for the planks, but after inspecting the quality of the trees, Purcell tells Norman and McIntosh, his mates, to cut down certain smaller trees of a different kind. When Bligh arrives to inspect the work, Purcell gets a verbal lashing by the captain because he did not follow the captain's *exact* orders. When Purcell tries to explain why he chose the smaller trees instead of the larger ones, Bligh calls him "a mutinous old bastard" and orders him to the ship to spend fifteen days in irons.

Wrangling and discontent continue among the men because of

the scant food available, while Bligh meantime feasts on wild duck. During the stay in the bay, Dick Skinner sees a hollow log with bees swarming around it and believes that he can get some honey. He gets lost in the woods while looking for more honey, and his comrade Young is blamed for this misadventure. He receives 12 lashes while strapped to a gun on the quarterdeck. Skinner receives 24 lashes for getting lost.

On the fourth of September, the *Bounty* sets sail and enters the South Sea seven weeks later, its crew miserable because of an outbreak of scurvy and a constant state of starvation. Byam sorts through his chest, anticipating trading with the Indians of Tahiti so that they can help him formulate his dictionary.

Captain Bligh asks Fryer, the master, to sign his name to an inventory list of what stores have been expended on the voyage thus far, but Fryer refuses because of discrepancies of the amount of beef and pork that have been issued to the men. Bligh calls all the men together on deck and orders Fryer to sign. Fryer signs the document, but not before saying to Bligh that "the ship's people will bear witness that I sign in obedience to your orders, but please to recollect, sir, that this matter may be reopened later on."

Tahiti is sighted in the foreground.

Commentary

As noted previously, Chapter 3 emphasizes the crowded conditions that the men must live under, conditions that will impair not only their physical existence, but their mental health as well. Chapter 3 also emphasizes the fact that the men aboard the *Bounty* are all first-rate men. The officers and the midshipmen are either "men of good birth" or "first-rate seamen and navigators." Likewise, the able seamen are among the best seamen that any captain might obtain. Historically speaking, on such a mission as the *Bounty*'s, the seamen would normally *not* be a quality crew; they would be "impressed" into duty from jails and low-class taverns—in short, they would be the "scum of the sea." Therefore, we should remember that the mutiny will not be carried out by low-class criminals but, instead, by highly respected seamen who were pushed beyond the point of endurance.

In contrast to the other characters on board ship is the surgeon who, because of his wooden leg and his penchant for alcoholic beverage, is a comic figure, functioning mainly as comic relief in the movie versions of this novel.

Chapter 3 begins to plant the "seeds of discontent" that will later lead to the mutiny. We should always remember that there is not a *single* cause for the mutiny; instead, there is a multiplicity of causes that culminate in the mutiny. For example, at the first stop, Teneria, the crew's allotment of salt beef is replaced by fresh beef that is too foul to eat. A short time later, the crew discovers that Captain Bligh, in collusion with his clerk, Mr. Samuel, is deliberately withholding supplies from the crew in order to increase their own hoard. This is illustrated by the fifty pounds of cheese that Captain Bligh maintains was stolen. The members of the crew know that the cheese was taken to Bligh's home before the voyage began. This type of "smallness of mind" and "meanness" turn the men against Bligh. It is even rumored that some of the so-called fresh meat might be from indentured slave laborers, thus introducing the repugnant subject of cannibalism, a perversion particularly repellent to the crew members.

The terrible condition of the food is humorously illustrated at the end of Chapter 3, when one of the able seamen carves what seems to be a little wooden box. The substance that he is carving from turns out to be a tough piece of meat – a sample of the meat which the men are supposed to eat.

Chapter 4 is aptly titled "Tyranny" because it reveals Bligh to be a complete and irrational tyrant. From the very beginning of the voyage, Bligh can find nothing good to say about anyone on the ship. His neuroticism causes him to believe that the only way to control the men is by frequent threats of extreme punishment. He refuses even to consider Fletcher Christian's point of view that some Englishmen are best controlled by kindness.

The episode of the pumpkins, which are given out to replace the spoiled bread, is additional proof of Bligh's tyranny over the men. Once more, we see an illustration of the severity of "sea law." Bligh tells the men, "I am the only judge of .vhat is right and wrong. . . . The first man to complain from now on will be seized up and flogged." The men know that there will be no redress from Bligh's harsh discipline until the end of the voyage.

Other examples of Bligh's irrational behavior and inhuman treatment of his men include Mills' flogging because of the fresh shark incident, Tinkler's being sent to the masthead because of a boyish prank at night, Purcell's punishment because he chose different trees for the planks than those chosen by Bligh, Skinner's extreme punishment for inadvertently getting lost, and Young's unjust punishment for having been in charge of the honey-gathering expedition.

- **old-style Navy salt** an experienced sailor.

- **the bos'n's whistle** the boatswain's whistle.

- **grog** watered-down rum.

- **duff** a stiff, spicy pudding.

- **adze** a heavy, curved tool for dressing timbers.

- **snuggery** a snug, cozy, private room.

- **purser** the officer aboard ship in charge of money.

- **the cooper** the person who repairs casks and barrels.

- **squalls** sudden, violent gusts of rain and strong wind.

- **hove-to** to bring a ship to a standstill without anchoring.

- **firked** whacked, or smacked.

- **a fortnight** a period of two weeks.

- **a fowling piece** a light gun used for shooting birds.

- **scurvy** a disease caused by a lack of vitamin C, characterized by swollen, bleeding gums, livid spots, and prostration.

CHAPTERS 5-7

Summary

Having traveled more than twenty-seven thousand miles, the *Bounty* finally drops anchor in Matavai Bay. Many canoes from the island sail out to meet the ship, and Bligh advises Byam to choose a highly placed Tahitian as his *taio*, or friend, so that Byam can have the best possible help as he compiles his dictionary. Byam chooses Hitihiti, a chieftain, as his *taio*, and Hitihiti accepts the offer. Then the chieftain asks Bligh where Captain Cook is. Bligh lies, telling him that he (Bligh) is the son of Captain Cook, and he refrains from adding that Cook is dead. Later, Bligh instructs the *Bounty*'s crew never to mention Cook's death.

Hitihiti takes Byam to his house on Tahiti, a magnificent building sixty feet long by twenty feet wide, with a floor of fresh white coral sand, spread with mats. We meet Hitihiti's daughter, Hina, a woman of grace and beauty; Maimiti, niece of Hitihiti; and Hina's husband. Byam eats a meal of baked fish, pork, bananas, and coconut pudding with his host before falling asleep on the mats.

Next day, Byam begins to formulate the dictionary and discovers the many rich intricacies of the Tahitian language. Hitihiti and his household generously help Byam in his task, and Byam reports weekly to Bligh aboard the *Bounty* concerning the progress made. Bligh orders a large tent pitched on the island to shelter the breadfruit trees which Mr. Nelson and his assistants are gathering. Discipline on board the *Bounty* is relaxed, and the men are frequently allowed to go ashore for pleasure.

Christian, Peckover (the gunner) and Huggan (the surgeon) join Byam on the island one day, and later, Christian, Hina, Maimiti, and Byam go for a swim. Christian is greatly attracted to Maimiti, and walking back to Hitihiti's house, they hold hands. Christian continues to visit Maimiti on the island and soon is accepted by Hitihiti's household as her lover.

Through Christian, Byam learns that the surgeon died after eating a poisonous fish. He is buried on the island, but not before Nelson, Peckover, and Byam have one final drink by his grave in his memory.

It is not long before discipline on board the *Bounty* becomes less lax. Each man is required, on boarding the ship, to give up whatever gifts he has received from his *taio*. The gifts are to be disposed of as the captain sees fit. Despite the fact that many hogs are in the hold below, the men are still rationed a small portion of stale pork by Mr. Samuel.

At the gangway, Christian is ready to board the ship carrying hogs, fine mats, Indian cloths, and a pair of pearls. Bligh orders Christian to give the gifts to Mr. Samuel. Christian hesitantly does so but refuses to relinquish the pearls. Then he goes below deck with the pearls, and nothing more is said.

The crew begins mumbling in their ranks about the harsh conditions on board the ship and also about Bligh's refusal to increase their allowance of food. Upon boarding the *Bounty* for his weekly report to Bligh, Byam learns that William Muspratt and John Millward, both able seamen, and Charles Churchill, the master-at-arms, have deserted. Bligh orders Byam and some of the other men to search for the deserters in one of Hitihiti's canoes. Hitihiti and a dozen of his men accompany Byam, but the search is futile, so the expedition stops at Rimatuu, an islet, for the night. While there, they attend a ceremony held by the local Indians, and Byam notices a lovely woman and asks who she is. Hitihiti tells Byam that her name is Tehani and that she is a descendant of great ancestry. Spellbound, Byam watches her throughout the entire ceremony.

Upon returning to the *Bounty* the next day, Byam informs Captain Bligh that the three deserters cannot be found. Three weeks later, however, they give themselves up and are punished: Churchill receives two dozen lashes, and Muspratt and Millward get four dozen each.

The crew learns that the *Bounty* is ready to set sail, and, not surprisingly, those who have formed relationships with women on the island are troubled and melancholy. As scheduled, the *Bounty* sails for the West Indies with the breadfruit trees stored in the great cabin, leaving Tahiti in their wake.

Commentary

These chapters present an idyllic interlude on the beautiful South Sea island of Tahiti, often referred to both in the novel and in real life as a "paradise on earth." The contrast between the severity of the ship and the beautiful serenity of the island life will make the conditions aboard ship even more precipitous. The acceptance of the men by the people of Tahiti lulled the seamen into a life of peace and serenity, especially because most of the seamen were able to find a suitable woman to live with. The fact that some of the seamen became extremely attached to their Polynesian women is another motivating factor in the mutiny. Byam, of course, was allowed to indulge in total freedom in order to formulate his dictionary, and he became so proficient that he is convinced that he is the only white man who is able to speak the Tahitian language fluently. This talent, or facility, with the language will tempt him to return to these beautiful islands — even after he has been exonerated of all guilt in the court-martial before the Lord High Admiral of Great Britain.

Chapter 6 essentially gives a full description of the type of life and living conditions on the island; except for these facts, though, the chapter does not move the novel forward.

Chapter 7 renews the conflict between Christian and Bligh. During the interlude at Tahiti, Byam has come to know Christian much better and has developed an admiration for the man – partly because of Christian's becoming Maimiti's lover. Byam's admiration of Christian will allow Byam to more easily sympathize with Christian's unjust treatment, but it will not extend to Byam's joining Christian later during the mutiny.

The death of the surgeon, fondly called Old Bacchus after the classical god of wine, presents a foreboding note. Earlier, he was able to enliven the men's spirits; now, in his absence, the morale of the men on board ship will suffer. All of these minor occurrences will contribute to the mutiny later in the novel.

Captain Bligh's mean-spirited behavior, as well as his miserliness, are again illustrated in his demand that *all* items given by the natives to the crew must be placed under the captain's "protection." The men are rightly suspicious that their personal property will become Bligh's personal property; thus the men carry even more hatred and animosity toward Bligh. This animosity increased due to the fact that even while the *Bounty* was anchored on the island, Bligh still imposed ridiculous rationing on the men who were on duty aboard ship: "In the midst of plenty, and treated like smugglers each time they returned from shore," the men seethed with anger and resentment against Bligh. Each of these events is a stepping stone, leading to the mutiny.

Such scenes as midshipman Hallet's reporting on Ellison, when Ellison brings a suckling pig aboard, align Hallet with Bligh's faction, and, consequently, after the mutiny, even though Hallet will beg to remain on board the ship, the rest of the men will force him into Bligh's boat – partly because he is as hateful and spiteful as Bligh. Note particularly that our opinion of Hallet is colored by Byam when he calls Hallet "a little swine."

The episode of Christian's being requested to turn over all of his gifts, including the lovely pearls which Maimiti gave him as a gift for his mother, once again tests Christian's patience with the captain. His refusal to obey Bligh causes a serious breach in their relationship. At this point, Byam observes, "It was not hard to imagine the feelings of the *Bounty's* crew – rationed in the midst of plenty, and treated like smugglers each time they returned from shore. . . . It seemed to me that if Mr. Bligh continued as he had begun, we should soon have desertions or worse." With Byam expressing such obvious, communal feelings about Bligh, it would seem to the casual reader that he would be among those who would join a mutiny, but this is *not* to be the case.

The mutiny is further anticipated by the fact that three of the men – Churchill, Muspratt, and Millward – try to desert the ship while they are in Tahiti. This attempt attests to the dreadful conditions under Bligh and to the men's frustration. Even Byam is reluctant to leave Tahiti; he dreads the return trip under the command of Bligh.

- **take a caulk** go close your eyes and rest.

- **outrigger** a small South Pacific sailboat with a wooden float extending outboard from the side of the boat for added stability.

- **bole** the stem or trunk of a tree.

- **siesta** a mid-day nap.

- **ennui** boredom.

- **orthography** spelling.

- **hundredweight** a weight equivalent to 100 pounds in the U.S., 112 pounds in England.

- **a brace of** a pair of, a couple.

- **a fashionable watering place** a gathering place where drinking water is obtained; a spring.

- **two old duennas** two old chaperones.

- **plantains** tropical fruit resembling bananas.

CHAPTERS 8 & 9

Summary

The *Bounty*'s crew performs its duties as usual, but there is little heartiness displayed. The men feel morose and resentful after leaving the idyllic life of Tahiti.

The island of Namuka, one of "The Friendly Islands," is sighted on April 23. It is on this island that Bligh hopes to replenish the ship's water and wood supply, but as soon as he sets foot on the island, the natives make trouble for the crew, and they are forced to hurry back to the boat. Bligh calls Christian a coward, and Christian abruptly leaves the deck.

The following day, after setting sail from Namuka, Bligh notices that some coconuts are missing. He orders all of the officers on deck and questions them. All deny knowledge of the missing coconuts. Bligh accuses the officers of shielding whoever is responsible, and, finally, he accuses Christian of having stolen the coconuts. Christian finds it incredible that Bligh (or any captain) would accuse his second-in-command of stealing. As a result of this coconut incident, the men's allowance of grog is cut off, and the yams are rationed from one pound per person to half a pound.

That evening, Byam and Tinkler realize that they can't sleep, so they go up on deck, and there, Tinkler admits to Byam that he stole *one* coconut and that Christian saw him, yet looked the other way. Tinkler falls asleep by a quarter-deck gun, just as Christian appears on deck to talk to Byam. He asks Byam to visit his family in England if he (Christian) doesn't make it back to England safely. Byam agrees, saying, "You can count on me." At this moment, Bligh interrupts the two men, putting an end to their conversation. Tinkler and Byam return to their berths below, Tinkler complaining to Byam that he got no sleep on deck because Christian and Byam were talking and he overheard the entire conversation.

Byam is suddenly shaken awake the following morning and learns that the ship has been seized by several of the crew members. He and Stewart are forced on deck and are surprised to learn that Christian is taking part in the mutiny. Bligh has his hands tied behind his back and is taunted by some of the mutineers—in particular, by Churchill, Mills, Isaac Martin, Skinner, and Burkitt. Ellison is ecstatic, dashing about Bligh and flourishing a bayonet. The men beg Christian to slit Bligh's throat, but Christian refuses, saying that he plans to take Bligh back to England to be tried for conduct unbecoming an officer. The men refuse to let him take Bligh to England, and, at this point, Christian realizes that he must alter his plans.

Christian decides to set Bligh and his followers adrift in the *Bounty's* launch. He gives each man the opportunity to join Bligh, and Byam and Stewart, along with some other crewmen and officers, decide to go. Byam and Stewart are told to get their belongings, so they descend to their cabin. Meanwhile, the launch is supplied with food and water, navigational instruments, and a few tools.

While in their berths, Byam and Stewart decide to use some Indian clubs that they got at the Friendly Islands and overpower Thompson, their guard, but the plan is foiled when Burkitt and McCoy join Thompson in guarding the door. By the time the young men are escorted to the deck, the launch has already pushed off, heavily loaded with nineteen men, its top edge only seven or eight inches above the water. Byam, Stewart, Morrison, and the other men who took no part in the mutiny have no choice now: they must remain aboard the *Bounty*, along with the mutineers.

Commentary

The authors continue giving us evidence that Captain Bligh is an irrational tyrant and, in doing so, they seem to approve the mutiny. Even such loyal men as Mr. Nelson (the botanist), who is "truly called the salt of the earth" and who is "a rock of peace in our turbulent ship's company," confesses to Byam that had he been one of the sailors, he would have deserted the ship, taken to the hills, and remained in Tahiti.

Bligh is particularly (and publicly) rude to Fletcher Christian. When Christian returns from his expedition to the island and reports some losses, Bligh flies "into a rage, cursing him in language that would have been out of place had he been speaking to a common sailor." Bligh, of course, is so thick-skinned that he has no concept of how galling such remarks can affect a man of breeding and honor. It was understood at that time that a naval officer would *never*, under any circumstance, make a derogatory comment about a fellow officer in the presence of common sailors. To do so would be a terrible breach of ethics. Therefore, for Bligh to call Christian "an incompetent cowardly rascal," who is afraid of a "crowd of bloody savages" is a professional breach of ethics so profound that it helps us to better understand Christian's actions during the mutiny. That is, the captain so violates Christian's personal rights as a human being and as an officer that we can understand why Christian would feel justified in taking some kind of redress.

In any case of mutiny, much of the blame must be laid on the captain, even though mutiny is such a horror to a naval man that, during the court-martial, the unjust actions of the captain are virtually never brought out. We, however, know of Bligh's cruelty. In this chapter, Byam observes that Bligh often seems to be insane when he goes into one of his rages, and that he often works himself into a passion over trivial matters of little consequence. One such episode concerns the disappearance of the coconuts. This scene presents Bligh as an absolute maniac; again, he humiliates Christian, calling him a thief and inhumanely rationing the men's food – all because of his irrational desire for revenge.

Concerning the above episodes on board the *Bounty*, the captain's behavior can easily be compared to two other irrational captains in modern literature. In *The Caine Mutiny* and, to a lesser degree, in *Mister Roberts*, the men revolt against the captain because of his reaction to a trivial matter – the consumption of strawberries in the former and the moving of a plant in the latter. In each work, the captain is an unreasonable tyrant.

The end of Chapter 8 presents a scene that will be highly significant at the end of the novel. Here, young Tinkler and Byam are on deck talking, and Tinkler says that he is going to take a nap. Afterward, Byam talks with Fletcher Christian. The key to this scene is that Christian asks Byam to promise to explain matters to Christian's father – in case Christian never returns to England. At the moment that Byam promises Christian "You can count on me," Bligh arrives – just in time to overhear Byam's last comment. Later, Bligh will interpret that promise to mean that Byam had just told Christian that he could count on him to assist in the mutiny. The key to Byam's life, after he is judged guilty by a court-martial, lies in whether or not Tinkler can remember Byam's entire conversation with Christian. Here, Tinkler says that he was unable to sleep and *heard everything* they said. Later, however, will he be able to recall this seemingly insignificant conversation?

Chapter 9 is the central episode of the novel and, of course, gives the novel its title. Whereas on land, the word "treason" carries with it the strongest possible connotation of being the most despicable crime imaginable; likewise, aboard ship, "mutiny" is the highest possible crime. One doesn't mutiny for insignificant reasons, and yet after the mutiny has occurred, the reasons for the mutiny are hardly ever considered. Only the *act* of mutiny is significant; the mutineers are instantly guilty of a heinous crime. Significantly, the mutineers' motivation for committing the mutiny is seldom ever considered during their court-martial trials.

To repeat and belabor the point, mutiny is *the most contemptible and horrendous crime that can be committed at sea*. Consequently, many of the people who are sympathetic to the mutineers or who were outraged at Captain Bligh's intolerable and irrational behavior will nonetheless throw in their lot with the captain. The perfect example of this is Purcell, the carpenter, who, more than anyone else on the ship, despises the captain, even though he is regarded by the crew as "a tyrant second only to Bligh." However, he chooses to cast his lot with the dreaded and hateful Bligh rather than take part in a mutiny.

Ironically, in spite of the fact that Fletcher Christian will be considered a mutineer, a traitor, and a pirate (the ship he takes is the king's property), he is seen as a much more humane and decent captain than Bligh ever was. Left to their own devices, the able seamen who suffered so unjustly under the command of Captain Bligh would have eventually either brutalized or killed Bligh. It is paradoxical that Christian saves Bligh's life, enabling Bligh to retaliate, persecute, and condemn Christian later in the narrative.

Throughout the mutiny, there are bits and pieces of conversation which, if properly recalled, would have cleared Byam during this trial. For example, the first mate, Mr. Fryer, asks Mr. Byam, "Surely you are not concerned in this?" and Byam answers him, "No more than yourself, sir." Likewise, Mr. Nelson knows that he and Byam requested to be allowed to go with Bligh. Yet, according to sea law, all types of this kind of evidence are ignored, and the jury takes Bligh's word that Byam was part of the mutiny—in spite of all evidence to the contrary. Likewise, Hayward and Hallet, two of the midshipmen, *could* have testified on Byam's behalf because they were not only witnesses to Byam's wish to go with Bligh, but wanted to stay on the ship with Christian because of their cowardice. People such as Hayward and Hallet, who were "half-carried to the gangway" and who were "shedding tears and crying for mercy" and "clasping hands" and begging imploringly, "In God's name permit me to stay on the ship"— these kinds of people are *not* to be trusted; consequently, it is understandable that they wouldn't want to testify in Byam's behalf because their cowardice would be exposed.

- **Slit the dog's gullet!** slit the guy's throat!

- **the cutter** a small, single-masted boat.

- **the launch** a heavy, open-deck rowboat.

- **a sextant** an instrument used for measuring latitudes and longitudes.

- **the armourer** one who repairs firearms.

- **foundering** sinking.

- **calabashes of water** hollowed-out gourds filled with water.

- **a whiff of grape** smoke that follows a cannon blast of small, cast-iron balls, clustered together like grapes.

- **ten leagues distant** a league is roughly three miles.

- **Huzza for Tahiti!** Hurrah! Let's head for Tahiti!

CHAPTERS 10 & 11

Summary

Chapter 10 begins with a list of those who accompanied Bligh in the launch, a list of those who took an active part in the mutiny, and a list of those who remain on the *Bounty* but took no part in the mutiny. Roger Byam is included in this last group.

Christian stresses to his fellow mutineers the need for order on the ship and is elected captain. He tells the other men that they will be treated fairly—as long as they show no hostility towards the crew.

Christian then begins sailing the South Sea for an uninhabited island where the men of the *Bounty* can live. An island, Rarotonga, is sighted and approached, but the *Bounty* sails on.

Christian asks Byam into his cabin, and the two men talk about the mutiny. Christian tells Byam that it was not planned; it suddenly happened in a five-minute span. Byam learns further that Christian had planned to desert the ship on a raft built secretly by John Norton, the quartermaster, but because the weather was so calm, it thwarted his plan. Christian relates to Byam the sequence of events just prior to the seizure of the ship: how he had seen Hayward asleep at his watch, and how "as plainly as though they had been spoken, I heard the words 'Seize the ship!'"

On May 29, the ship arrives at an island believed to be Tupuai, discovered by Captain Cook. The islanders are hostile towards the *Bounty*, and the ship is soon forced to abandon all hopes of making a landing. Some of the mutineers want to turn the *Bounty*'s guns on the islanders, but Christian will have no part in this. He is resolved to make "a peaceful settlement or none at all." Christian then calls a meeting of the mutineers, and it is decided to sail for Tahiti.

Christian tells Byam that they are headed for Tahiti, but that those men who didn't participate in the mutiny won't be permitted to go ashore. Christian fears that they might persuade the Tahitians to attack the *Bounty*, or else try to escape and wait for an English ship to pick them up. The breadfruit trees stored in the great cabin are thrown overboard, and, meanwhile, Byam, Stewart, and Morrison talk about escape. In desperation, they make plans for Peggy, Stewart's Tahitian lover, to sneak up to the side of the *Bounty* in a canoe. They will then jump into it and escape.

On the fifth of June, the *Bounty* reaches Tahiti. The Tahitians are told that the *Bounty* met Captain Cook's ship, and that Bligh and other members of the crew, including the botanist, transferred the breadfruit trees to Cook's ship, the captain staying aboard his "father's vessel" while the *Bounty*, under Christian's command, returned to Tahiti for further trading.

Stewart talks with Peggy aboard the *Bounty*, and the two plan the escape, but the weather is so bad that there is no chance to escape before Christian orders the anchors raised, and the *Bounty* sails out of Matavi Bay.

The *Bounty*, now carrying the Tahitians who wished to join the men aboard, again sails towards Tupuai. The Tahitians persuade the Tupuai natives to let the sailors live on the island, but hostilities still exist. Growing tired of the constant fighting between themselves and the natives, the crew of the *Bounty* and the Tahitians leave the island. Sixteen of the crew want to be taken to Tahiti, so Christian acquiesces. Byam, Stewart, Morrison, and thirteen others are dropped off at Tahiti, and Christian and those who remain with him set sail in search of an uninhabited island to live out the remainder of their lives. Byam returns to live with Hitihiti.

Commentary

In Chapter 10, we learn almost as much about the enigmatic

Fletcher Christian as we are ever to know. Byam reports that he knows the man as well as anyone, but he feels that there is some hidden force driving Christian. Byam reports that Christian's "sense of the wrongs he suffered at Bligh's hands was so deep and overpowering as to dominate . . . every other feeling." Byam feels that Christian is a man of such passion that when he feels the extent of the injustice perpetrated against him, he loses all sense of everything—except his own misery.

After the mutiny, Christian becomes somewhat of a solitary man, yet he runs the ship efficiently and, unlike Bligh, with justice. He does not resort to petty flogging to satisfy his whims. Instead, he has a sense of justice that allows him to treat his men as human beings. Had Bligh possessed this attitude, the mutiny would never have occurred. Byam writes that "the absence of Bligh was a godsend to all of us, mutineers and non-mutineers alike. There was no more of the continual feeling of tension, of uncertainty as to what would happen . . . Christian maintained the strictest discipline, but no one had cause to complain of his justice." It is ironic that Christian is a born leader of men, yet due to the circumstances connected with the mutiny, he was never allowed to display that leadership.

Byam is surprised to discover that the mutiny was unplanned. Christian assures him that ten minutes before the mutiny, he had not even considered seizing Bligh, but instead had already collaborated with the ship's quartermaster to build him a small craft so he could desert the ship. Being a man of conscience, he regrets the fate that he has brought on others. Concerning Bligh, however, he has no regrets; Bligh is a man so sordid and so contemptible that there can be no pity for him.

When Byam and his companions discover that they won't be allowed to go ashore in Tahiti, they plan an escape. They have no idea that they have been accused of treason back in England, and it will, of course, be a shock to them when they discover this fact. Unfortunately, their plan to escape from the ship is foiled by the weather.

Chapter 11 brings a conclusion to the fate of the *Bounty*. For some fortunate (but unexplained) reasons, Byam and anyone who wishes to remain on Tahiti are allowed to do so.

- **the arms chest** the chest where the firearms are kept.

- **the barrier reef** a reef of coral running parallel to the shore and separated from it by deep water.

- **to come to naught** to fail.

- **King George** King George III of England; ruled for 60 years (1760–1820); his policies led to the American Revolution.

CHAPTERS 12 & 13

Summary

Byam meets Tehani, the beautiful princess he saw during his initial stay in Tahiti, and he falls deeply in love with her. The two marry and move into a house just below Tehani's uncle's house on the opposite side of the island from Hitihiti.

Byam continues to work on the Tahitian dictionary, and one day he and Tehani sail around the island to see Hitihiti, Stewart, and Morrison. Byam learns that Morrison, Norman, McIntosh, Muspratt, and Byrne are constructing a boat to take them to Batavai, where the chances are greater that they might be picked up by an English ship. Byam also learns where the other crewmen of the *Bounty* are living on Tahiti, and that Churchill has been killed by Thompson, who has also killed a Tahitian man and his child.

On the fifteenth of August, 1790, Tehani gives birth to a daughter, Helen, named after Byam's mother. Stewart and Peggy and their young daughter come to visit Tehani and Byam, and the group spend the day on an uninhabited area along the shore. Life on the island continues to be soothing for Byam, and all thoughts of England soon become only blurred memories.

Commentary

Any novel dealing with the South Sea is bound to have a romantic interlude in it. *Mutiny of the Bounty* is no exception. Byam's meeting the beautiful Tehani is presented in such perfect, idyllic terms that the reader cannot understand why Byam, or anyone, would want to leave this island paradise. Yet some of the men do become impatient with this seemingly perfect existence. Thompson, for no logical reason, kills a native and his child, and later kills Churchill before being killed by the natives; yet even this horror does not make any of the natives turn against the other Europeans. Later, writing about these times, Byam will maintain that these were the happiest eighteen months of his life.

- **a fathom deep** a unit of measurement equal to six feet.

- **retainers** old, loyal servants or employees.

- **nothing loath** not reluctantly.

- **throwing off his mantle** throwing off his cloak.

- **an isthmus** a narrow strip of land, bordered on both sides by water, connecting two large areas of land.

- **wild glen** a small, overgrown, secluded valley.

- **cumber my narrative** burden a story with unnecessary details.

CHAPTERS 14 & 15

Summary

Byam rows out to meet the arriving ship and learns that it is British, the *Pandora*, commanded by a Captain Edwards. After telling Edwards his name and that he was a midshipman aboard the *Bounty*, Byam is immediately locked in irons below deck and is told that Bligh reached England and told the proper authorities about the mutiny; more important, Bligh included Byam among the men who seized the *Bounty*. Byam maintains his innocence, but Edwards orders him to be silent. Hayward, on board the *Pandora*, is asked to identify Byam, which he does. On reaching the *Pandora*, Stewart, Joseph Coleman (the *Bounty*'s armorer), and Skinner are also shackled alongside Byam.

A few days after his imprisonment, Byam meets the *Pandora*'s doctor, Mr. Hamilton, in Hamilton's quarters. He learns that Bligh overheard Byam tell Christian "You can count on me" the night before the mutiny; this is why Bligh believes that Byam was one of the mutineers. However, Hamilton says, Sir Joseph Banks believes that Byam is innocent of the mutiny. Byam is then told that Norton, who could have testified on his behalf, was killed by savages on the island of Tofoa while accompanying Bligh back to England. Byam suddenly realizes that—now that Norton is dead—his innocence relies *completely* on Tinkler. Hamilton promises to ask Captain Edwards to let the shackled men be allowed to converse with each other, which they have been forbidden to do, and also to provide Byam with the means to continue his work on the Tahitian dictionary while the *Pandora* sails to England. He then gives Byam a letter from Sir Joseph Banks, in which Banks states his belief in Byam's innocence. Hamilton also shows Byam a letter which Bligh wrote to Byam's mother, in which he accuses Byam of mutiny, saying, "His baseness is beyond all description."

Commentary

Throughout these sections, the authors continually introduce matters that in a modern court of law would offer themselves as extenuating circumstances, or mitigating events. For example, in modern jurisprudence (legal matters), if a guilty person voluntarily surrenders himself, it is a point in his favor. Here, it should be obvious that if Byam *were* guilty of mutiny, he would *never* have reported to the *Pandora* and offered to help guide her to a safe anchoring. Yet at the court martial, this action has no bearing on the trial. Consequently, to understand the apparent total disregard for basic logic and basic psychological motivation, we have to return to the second chapter of the novel, "Sea Law," in which it is made clear that the laws of the sea are strict, unbending, and completely authoritarian. According to sea law, at a court-martial there can be nothing under consideration except the captain's word, and, as we will see later, in a great travesty of justice, the captain is not even present to be cross-examined. The judges are not concerned with the captain's injustices, his acts of inhumanity, his criminality, or his brutality. Upholding "sea law" is the most important factor to the judges.

Byam knows that he is innocent, and therefore he is horrified to find that he has been accused of mutiny. It is not until the good and humane Dr. Hamilton explains the reason for Byam's captivity that Byam realizes the severity of his situation. As noted, Bligh overheard Byam say to Christian, "You can count on me." This single sentence, uttered to Christian by Byam, will condemn Byam to death because of the inexorable law of the sea and the supposed infallibility of a captain's pronouncement. At present, these words are enough to put Byam in chains and placed in a smelly, filthy hole in the ship.

Hallet (later on in the novel) or Hayward (in Chapter 14) could have defended Byam or spoken up in his behalf, but because they need to conceal their own cowardice, they choose to send an innocent man to his death.

Byam's alleged crime seems even more horrible because, in addition to the gravity of the mutiny, Captain Bligh performed a navigational feat that could never have been accomplished by anyone except a truly extraordinary man. He navigated his men over thirty-six hundred miles of rough sea in an open boat with hardly any food or water – and with virtually no navigational equipment. Thus, because of the magnificence of this feat, Bligh becomes a national hero. His name becomes synonymous with British superiority at a time when, historically, the British were in need of a strong rallying point.

- **an English frigate** a small, fast naval ship, heavily armed.

- **orlop deck** the lowermost deck at the bottom of the ship.

- **sentinels** watchmen, or guards.

- **the Admiralty** the Department of the Navy.

- **baseness** cowardice; having despicable qualities.

- **scuttles** small hatches or openings in the deck.

CHAPTERS 16 & 17

Summary

The following morning, Captain Edwards enters the prisoners' cell and orders Lieutenant Parkin to inform the men that they may converse – but only in English. He then leaves the cell and Parkin checks Stewart's irons by having Stewart lie on his back while Parkin steps on his chest and pulls sharply on the irons. The irons rip the skin off the backs of Stewart's hands and knuckles; he attempts to lunge at Parkin but is unsuccessful because of the irons around his ankles. Tighter irons are put on Stewart.

The four men are moved on deck into a roundhouse, eleven feet long and eighteen feet wide. Two days later, Morrison, Norman, and Ellison are placed in the roundhouse, having been captured by the *Pandora's* launch, headed by Hayward. McIntosh, Hillbrandt, Burkitt, Millward, Sumner, Muspratt, and Byrne are also brought into the roundhouse and shackled; they were captured on the island of Papara, where Morrison, Norman, and Ellison were captured earlier.

Dr. Hamilton visits the men in the roundhouse, and they ask him if they might have fresh food instead of salt beef and hard bread. Hamilton is taken aback, thinking that the prisoners have been receiving fresh food. It is apparent to the men that Captain Edwards and Hamilton have no idea of the cruel conditions that Lieutenant Parkin is imposing on the men.

Dr. Hamilton takes Byam and Stewart to the sick bay on the lower deck, where Tehani and Peggy are waiting with their daughters. Tehani and Peggy tell the two men that some of the Tahitians are planning to attack the *Pandora* in order to free the men, but Byam and Stewart tell them that it is futile to try, whereupon the two women burst into tears.

Dr. Hamilton persuades Captain Edwards to allow the prisoners to speak in Tahitian so that Byam can work on the Tahitian dictionary and gain from the conversation. The *Pandora* then leaves Tahiti in search of the *Bounty*.

The long days and nights spent in the roundhouse by the fourteen men begin to take their toll. Hillbrandt begins to pray constantly, even in the middle of the night, fearful of the court-martial that lies ahead. He can think of nothing but the court-martial: "We're doomed, men . . . doomed, every one of us! We're to be hanged, think of that! Choked to death at the end of a rope!"

The *Pandora* continues to search the South Sea for Christian and the *Bounty*, but after two months of finding no trace of her, except for a driver gaff, Captain Edwards decides to head back to England.

Commentary

Mutiny on the Bounty presents its characters essentially in black and white. That is, men like Bligh and Parkin are "black," meaning evil, while men like Dr. Hamilton and Sir Joseph Banks, who sends word to Byam that he believes in the innocence of the young boy, are meant to be seen as "white," meaning good and noble. If it weren't for the constant interference and watchful eye of Dr. Hamilton, it is doubtful that the prisoners would have reached England alive. Although Hamilton tries to defend Captain Edwards as a just man, Byam's opinion is that Edwards is cruel; we will see evidence of this during the shipwreck episode. Finally, even good Dr. Hamilton has to admit that men like Captain Edwards too often carry out the "letter" of the law and not the "spirit" of the law, causing unnecessary anguish and grief. However, Captain Edwards' behavior is mild in comparison with the deliberate malevolence of Lieutenant Parkin, who sadistically delights in inflicting punishment on the men.

It is interesting to note that at the end of Chapter 17, men such as Byam, Stewart, Morrison, Coleman, Norman, McIntosh, and Byrne (men who were opposed to the mutiny), now that they have been captured and are being treated in an inhumane way, desperately hope that the *Pandora* does *not* find Fletcher Christian and his crew of mutineers. Under such adverse treatment, their values have significantly altered.

- **manacles** handcuffs, or irons.

- **humours** ailments.

- **steward** the man in charge of domestic affairs aboard ship.

- **kicked from larboard to starboard** kicked from one side of the ship (the port, left-hand side) to the other (the right-hand side).

- **galled** chaffed, raw.

CHAPTERS 18 & 19

Summary

On its journey home, the *Pandora* strikes ground and instantly water rushes on board. The *Pandora's* crew makes haste to get rid of the water, while the prisoners beg to be freed of their irons to help bail, but Edwards refuses, increasing their guard two-fold. As the *Pandora* is sinking, a crewman jumps in the roundhouse and unshackles the prisoners. Some of the men of the *Pandora* reach safety in smaller boats, but many of them drown because they don't know how to swim.

The small boats come to rest on a sandbar, and of the prisoners, Stewart, Sumner, Hillbrandt, and Skinner are missing and presumed drowned. Tents are made from salvaged sails to shelter the crew, but Edwards refuses to allow the surviving prisoners any shelter under the tents.

Captain Edwards orders the *Pandora's* carpenters to repair the damage done to the small boats so that they can attempt to reach the island of Timor, where it is very likely that they will be picked up by an English ship. After the boats are repaired, the group sets out and reaches the Australian coastline after a day's journey. Only the crew of the *Pandora* is allowed to go ashore, where they find a spring to quench their frenzied thirst. The prisoners are forced to remain on the boats until Edwards decides to allow them to go ashore for water.

The boats set out the following day and find an island, but their attempt to land is abandoned after they encounter a hoard of unfriendly jet-black savages on the island's beach. The boats then head for another island and discover it to be uninhabited. Relevantly, Edwards sends Byam and Morrison in search of food because his own men can find nothing more than a few sea snails. The two men return to the camp loaded with lobsters, fish, and mussels. The group stays on the island, which Edwards names "Laforey's Island," for two days before embarking.

The lack of water affects the men greatly. One man offers all of his money to another man for one day's water allowance. Some of the men become so thirsty that they drink their own urine and die shortly thereafter.

After thirteen days at sea, the four boats reach the island of Timor, where the prisoners are taken to the fort in Coupang and put in stocks under Lieutenant Parkin's care.

After a very brief detainment in Timor, the prisoners are put aboard a ship bound for Batavia, and, upon reaching Batavia, they are transported to another ship, along with Captain Edwards and the crew of the *Pandora*, headed for the Cape of Good Hope. From the Cape of Good Hope, the ship *Gorgon* takes Byam and his fellow prisoners, as well as Edwards and his crew, to England, arriving on the nineteenth of June in Portsmouth Harbor. Four years and six months have passed since the departure of the *Bounty*, and during that time, Byam and the other prisoners have spent nearly fifteen months in chains.

Commentary

The cruelty of Captain Edwards is vividly evident in these chapters. However, we must remember that he has been charged with the duty of apprehending mutinous criminals and bringing them back to England to stand trial. To Edwards, these men are the basest felons imaginable—they revolted against their captain—and, as a captain himself, Edwards has a vested interest in seeing these men dutifully hanged in England as an example to any seaman who might consider mutiny. On the other hand, today's readers have difficulty fathoming his deliberate cruelty and comprehending why Edwards would leave the men locked in the sinking ship, as well as why he would leave the men totally exposed to the blistering sun—especially when there is an unused sail lying nearby which could have given them protection.

Chapter 19 contains the essence of the boring tedium during the long journey home, sparked by only a few unusual occasions. On one such occasion, the prisoners are responsible for literally saving the other sailors from starvation because they learned how to fish and survive in a primitive situation while they lived on Tahiti. Despite this generosity, however, they are still treated brutally. Likewise, the superb ship that several of the prisoners built is sold for a nice profit, but, again, the prisoners are without rights and receive no benefit from the sale. Significantly, the exhausted prisoners are treated decently by the Dutch captain—to the chagrin of Captain Edwards.

- **three feet [of water] in the hold**   three feet of water in the cargo space between the lowermost deck and the bottom of the ship.

- **a small sandy key**   a reef, or low island; also spelled *cay*.

- **a gill of wine**   one-fourth pint.

- **pinnace**   a light sailing vessel, especially one used in attendance on a larger vessel.

- **lay-to**   to check the motion of a ship.

- **the blue yawl**   a small, two-masted boat, usually manned by four oarsmen.

- **latitude**   the angular distance north or south from the equator on the earth's surface.

- **longitude**   the angular distance east or west on the earth's surface.

- **booby**   a tropic seabird; two of the most common boobies are the red-footed booby and the blue-footed booby.

- **placed in stocks**   placed in a wooden framework with holes for securing the wrists and ankles in order to expose a person to public ridicule.

- **extenuating circumstances**   circumstances which make a fault seem less serious.

- ***H.M.S. Gorgon***   *His Majesty's Ship Gorgon*

CHAPTERS 20 & 21

Summary

After arriving in Portsmouth, the prisoners are transferred to the *H.M.S. Hector*. Within an hour, Byam is taken to the captain's cabin, where he is allowed to read a letter from Sir Joseph Banks, which informs him that his mother is dead. Sir Joseph visits Byam a few days later and is excited to learn that Byam's Tahitian transcripts are intact and being kept by the *Pandora*'s doctor. Sir Joseph tells Byam that Bligh has sailed on another journey and that Bligh's sworn deposition is in the hands of the British Admiralty. Before leaving, Sir Joseph promises to find Tinkler, the one living man who can corroborate Byam's testimony.

Ten days pass, and Byam receives a letter from Sir Joseph informing him that Tinkler sailed on a ship headed for the West Indies, and that the ship was lost in a hurricane near the island of Cuba. Sir Joseph has talked to Fryer and some of the other men who sailed in the launch with Bligh, and these men will testify at Byam's trial. Also, Sir Joseph has found an able attorney to represent Byam, a Mr. Graham.

Mr. Graham visits Byam and the other men and encourages them not to give up hope. Morrison tells Mr. Graham that he will be representing himself before the tribunal.

Two months pass as the prisoners wait to be called before the court that will decide life or death for them.

Finally, on September 12, the prisoners are transferred aboard the *H.M.S. Duke*, the ship where the court-martial trials will be held. The audience at the tribunal includes Sir Joseph Banks, Captain Edwards of the *Pandora*, Dr. Hamilton of the *Pandora*, and the officers of the ill-fated *Bounty*. The sworn deposition of Captain William Bligh is read before the court, and, in it, Bligh accuses Byam of mutiny — based on Byam's statement the night preceding the mutiny: "You can count on me." This he said to Christian, to which Christian replied, "Good! That's settled, then."

John Fryer is called to testify before the tribunal. Fryer relates to the court the events leading up to the mutiny as best he knows. Fryer recalls that he asked Christian if Byam had any part in the mutiny, and Christian said that Byam did not. The prisoners are then allowed to question Fryer. Byam asks Fryer if he heard any of the conversation that Byam and Christian had the night preceding the mutiny, to which Fryer responds, "No." Byam also asks Fryer if he would have included Byam in a plan to retake the *Bounty*, to which Fryer responds that he would have.

Mr. Cole, the *Bounty*'s boatswain, is called to testify. His testimony is very unfavorable for Ellison, but unimportant to Byam's case. Cole's testimony helps Morrison's case the most. Cole points out that Morrison played absolutely no role in the mutiny and that, in fact, Morrison helped Bligh and Bligh's followers into the launch.

The court adjourns for the day, and the prisoners are taken back to the *Hector*, where Mr. Graham consults with Byam and asserts his belief that Byam is innocent of the mutiny.

Commentary

After the presentation of such horrible sea captains as Captain Bligh and Captain Edwards, we are suddenly and favorably exposed to a humanitarian captain in the person of Montague, captain of the *Hector*, who seems to be genuinely concerned about Byam's welfare, and, even more important, who treats Byam as though Byam were innocent rather than as an already-convicted felon.

Likewise, we again meet another good humanitarian in the person of Sir Joseph Banks, who fortunately holds an influential position as president of the Royal Society. He never loses his faith in Byam's honesty and integrity. While being sympathetic to Byam's predicament, Sir Joseph's comments about the case allow both the reader and Byam to realize fully, for the first time, the ultimate seriousness of Byam's position. That is, two of the people who can confirm Byam's story—Nelson and Norton—are dead, and another, Tinkler, is missing and presumed dead. Byam's position seems even worse because of the severity of sea law (see Chapter 2). Any person who "stands neuter is considered an offender along with the person who actually lifts his hand against the captain." This law will, of course, condemn

Ellison to death because not only did he *not* oppose the mutiny, but in his youthful exuberance, he delighted in waving a bayonet under Captain Bligh's nose.

In Chapter 21 and, ultimately, throughout the trial, we see many things which Byam can never forgive Bligh for doing. These include the unnecessarily cruel letter which Bligh wrote to Byam's mother, and Bligh's injustice to some of the men whom Bligh knows to be innocent. In view of the innocence of some of the men, Bligh's duplicity and vengeance is further illuminated since Bligh knew full well that such men as Coleman, Norman, and McIntosh desired to go with him but were *forcibly* restrained by the mutineers. "The barest justice demanded that he [Bligh] should have acknowledged their innocence, yet he made no distinction between them and the guiltiest members of Christian's party." This injustice Byam cannot comprehend.

In any court of law except a military court-martial, Mr. Fryer's testimony would probably provide ample evidence to clear Byam. Mr. Fryer – a man whose integrity and loyalty cannot be doubted – testifies that Byam had "no hand in this business." Later, Fryer repeats that Byam's actions were performed in order to assist Captain Bligh, and Byam, in cross-examining Fryer, reconfirms that he had *no part whatsoever* in the mutiny. And yet, all of the testimony in favor of Byam will be of no consequence in the face of the now-famous Captain Bligh's vindictively sworn statement.

- **tacked** to change the course of a sailing ship, or boat.
- **four cutlasses** four short, heavy, slightly curved swords.
- **binnacle** the stand that houses a ship's compass.

CHAPTERS 22 & 23

Summary

The court-martial is reconvened aboard the *Duke*, and William Peckover, the gunner of the *Bounty*, is called to the stand. Morrison questions Peckover after the court is finished with its examination, and Peckover testifies that he never once saw Morrison under arms and that Morrison did everything in his power to see that the launch had provisions and much-needed articles.

Purcell, the carpenter, is next called to the stand and testifies that it was Byam who persuaded Christian to give Bligh the *Bounty's* launch instead of the cutter, which was in bad repair. Purcell asserts that Byam is definitely innocent of all charges against him. Purcell affirms the court's question of whether Purcell believes that Christian would have told Byam of his plan to seize the *Bounty*, considering the fact that Byam was Christian's closest friend aboard the ship. Purcell, under questioning by Byam, describes the condition of the launch, how its edges were barely above water, and confirms that this is why Byam and some of the other men were *not* allowed to board the launch.

The following morning, Thomas Hayward gives his testimony. He relates the events leading up to the mutiny, and his testimony is very unfavorable for Byam's case. Hayward maintains that Byam *would not* have joined Bligh in the launch – even if he had been given the chance to do so.

John Hallet, called to the stand next, relates to the court that, at one point, Byam was standing by Bligh (who was bound), laughed in Bligh's face, and walked away. Hallet maintains further that Morrison was one of the mutineers and that he brandished a musket after the mutiny occurred.

John Smith, the only one of the *Bounty's* seamen to testify at the court-martial, is called to the stand, but he relates nothing of importance concerning Byam, Morrison, or any of the other prisoners. This concludes the evidence provided to the court by members of the *Bounty*. Captain Edwards and the lieutenants of the *Pandora* are next called upon to testify about the *Pandora's* journey after leaving Tahiti. Edwards testifies that Byam and the other men gave themselves up voluntarily by rowing out to meet the *Pandora* and identified themselves immediately. The court adjourns in anticipation of hearing the testimony of the prisoners the following day.

Coleman is the first to testify in his own behalf, and the questions that he asks of the other prisoners, as well as his own statements, leave no doubt that he will be acquitted. The court adjourns for the day.

When the court convenes Monday morning, Byam presents his defense. He reads a passionate statement concerning his innocence and relates to the court the circumstances and events leading up to the mutiny. Byam calls John Fryer to the stand and, in an attempt to discredit the testimony of Hayward and Hallet (given earlier), he questions Fryer about the emotional condition of the two men at the time of the mutiny. Fryer does so and also relates to the court what Bligh said about Byam after the launch had been set adrift.

Byam then proceeds to question Cole, Purcell, and Peckover, hoping that they will confirm that Tinkler overheard the conversation between Christian and Byam, and that the conversation had nothing whatsoever to do with the mutiny, but the three men cannot confirm Byam's testimony. Peckover does, however, remember having talked to Norton the night before the mutiny, and he also recalls that Norton was engaged in building what Peckover thought might have been a raft, but Peckover is unable to verify Byam's assertion that the raft was being built for Christian's use.

Morrison is called next to present his defense. His testimony goes very well, and he is even able to get Hayward and Hallet to admit that they *might* have been mistaken when they testified that they had seen him under arms.

Norman, McIntosh, and Byrne (the half-blind seaman) testify next, and it is clearly established that they are innocent of the charge of mutiny against the *Bounty*. Burkitt, Millward, and Muspratt take the stand in their own behalf, and it is evident that the first two played an active role in the mutiny. Ellison follows these three men with his brief statement.

The court adjourns and the prisoners are taken back to the *Hector* to await the court's verdict.

Commentary

These chapters are arranged around the basic drama of courtroom testimony; the outcome of the trial is pre-determined, except that we, as modern readers, know of Byam's innocence and expect that he will receive an acquittal of all charges. It is only when we look back and consider the sternness and absolute rigidity of naval courts and the authoritarian despotism of a captain at that time in history, do we then realize that Bligh's condemning statement as to the guilt of Byam and the other prisoners supersedes any other considerations.

Ironically, both chapters present further evidence of Byam's innocence. For example, Purcell, who hated Bligh as much as anyone on board the *Bounty*, testifies strongly in Byam's behalf, and he likewise maintains that Christian was *not* a person to reveal his thoughts to another person; consequently, Byam would know nothing of Christian's plans. Even the negative criticism offered by Hayward and Hallet is not convincing because their testimonies are given so as to conceal the fact that they were thoroughly terrified throughout the entire mutiny and reluctantly joined Bligh.

John Hallet's testimony can be readily dismissed by the reader because Byam knows of Hallet's sucking sychophantism. For example, in Chapter 8, Byam caught Hallet betraying a fellow crewman and called him a "little swine" and a "contemptible little sneak." Now, however, this is Hallet's chance for revenge, an opportunity to protect himself from the possibility that his cowardice might be revealed.

In Chapter 23, Byam makes his defense and selectively makes his cross-examinations, a defense which to the modern reader proves his innocence. For example, Byam does not even bother to cross-examine Hallet; instead, he questions Mr. Fryer about Hallet's actions during the mutiny so that Fryer's testimony will undermine Hallet's.

- **the taffrail** the rail around the stern (the front) of a ship.

- **like the thrust of a rapier** like the thrust of a small sword having a narrow blade, used for thrusting and slashing.

CHAPTERS 24 & 25

Summary

The prisoners are taken to the *Duke* while the members of the court deliberate and discuss the evidence against the men. Byam is then called into the great cabin, and the court announces that he is guilty of mutiny against the *Bounty* and that he is to be hanged. Morrison also receives the death penalty. Coleman, Norman, McIntosh, and Byrne are acquitted of all charges. Burkitt, Ellison, Millward, and Muspratt are called into the great cabin and all are found guilty and condemned to death. Morrison is called into the great cabin once again and is told that he has been recommended to His Majesty's mercy. The guilty men are taken back to the *Hector* to await the day that they will be hanged.

Sir Joseph comes to see Byam, bringing with him Byam's manuscript of the Tahitian dictionary. Byam is informed that he can work on the dictionary to help keep his mind busy if he so desires, which he does. Sir Joseph once again asserts that had Tinkler been present to give his testimony, Byam would have been acquitted of all charges. Before Sir Joseph leaves, he tells Byam that there is a possibility that Muspratt might still be cleared of the charge of mutiny.

While the men await the day that they are to be hanged, Dr. Hamilton comes to see Byam, and while the two are talking, Sir Joseph enters the room excitedly. Sir Joseph informs Byam that Tinkler has been found alive and that he is in London at that very moment. Byam learns further from Sir Joseph that Tinkler will be brought before Admiral Hood and that he will be questioned about the conversation between Christian and Byam the night before the mutiny. Dr. Hamilton and Sir Joseph then leave the ship.

A few days later, an armed guard comes to the room where the prisoners are being held and takes Burkitt, Millward, and Ellison away. The following day, Byam, Muspratt, and Morrison watch from their room as Burkitt, Millward, and Ellison are rowed to another boat on which they are to be hanged. While waiting to see the men hanged, Captain Montague of the *Hector* enters the room and informs Muspratt and Morrison that they have been granted mercy and that they are free to go. Captain Montague then informs Byam that Tinkler's testimony has been heard by Admiral Hood and that the charge of mutiny against Byam has been dropped.

On their way to Portsmouth Harbor, Byam, Morrison, and Muspratt are rowed past the ship on which Burkitt, Millward, and Ellison are to be hanged. A great gun breaks the silence, and as Byam looks back, he sees the bodies of the three men suspended in mid-air, twitching as they sway from side to side.

On the way to London, Byam is informed in a letter from Sir Joseph that a Mr. Erskine, a friend of Byam's deceased father, would like Byam to stay at his home for awhile. Byam, Muspratt, and Morrison part ways once they reach London, and Byam heads for Mr. Erskine's residence.

Tinkler is waiting for Byam, and he relates the events leading up to his testimony before Admiral Hood. The two eat supper and retire for the evening.

Commentary

Chapter 24 is one of the more emotional and suspenseful chapters of the novel. The scene is built around the verdict, and all of the people whom Byam knows and likes (Sir Joseph, Dr. Hamilton, Mr. Erskine, and Mr. Graham) are gathered to hear it. The reader has been led to hope that all of the extenuating testimony will bring about a verdict of acquittal for Byam, and we are shocked and stunned to discover that the verdict is "guilty" and that Byam is to be hanged. It is interesting how Byam receives this news. It is as though he were in a catatonic state. Only later will the full horror of this terrible ignominy be fully grasped.

At present, Byam's main concern focuses on the injustice that has been perpetrated against Morrison, who was convicted solely upon the unreliable and spiteful testimony of Hayward and Hallet.

Captain Montague's kindness towards Byam and his attempt to make Byam's present situation as endurable as possible, even to the point of granting him a personal cabin, is instrumental in causing Byam to change his mind later about returning to Tahiti.

Once again, in this scene, the complete authority and despotism of a sea captain is emphasized. Bligh's accusation is unquestioned, and, as expressed by Sir Joseph, is clearly the penultimate, unexonerated law of the seas. To quote Sir Joseph:

> There was no alternative, Byam. None. All the palliating circumstances – the fact that no man had seen you under arms, the testimony as to the excellent character you bore, and all the rest – were not sufficient to offset Bligh's damning statement as to your complicity with Christian in planning the mutiny. That statement stood unchallenged, except by yourself, throughout the court-martial.

Regardless of how corrupt, vindictive, evil, irrational or neurotic a captain may be, his word is the supreme authority, and his absolute power is unquestioned.

Byam's only comfort during his imprisonment is that the people whom he admires still believe in his innocence. Sir Joseph brings him the manuscript which will, in effect, keep him alive for another month, and Mr. Graham and Dr. Hamilton both visit him before leaving on another tour of duty.

The chapter ends with a sudden reversal. In literary terms, this technique is often criticized as a *deus ex machina* – literally, a "god in a machine." This means that the reader is not prepared for a sudden change of events, something that happens which has no motivation. In terms of this novel, we have been led to believe that Tinkler is dead; when he is suddenly "resurrected," the conclusion or resolution of the novel seems to have been brought about by artificial means. However, this device does satisfy the reader's demand for justice, and given the nature of the authoritarianism of sea law, Byam's life can be saved only by bringing back to life the presumably dead Tinkler. This technique could be further criticized in that we have not seen or known enough about Tinkler to be assured that he is the type who could intellectually and accurately reconstruct the conversation between Christian and Byam on the critical night.

After we hear the results of Tinkler's testimony, we witness the execution of Burkitt, Millward, and Ellison. By the laws of the time — humane or inhumane, though they may be — no reader can argue about the guilt of Burkitt and Millward — that is, even if one is opposed to the death penalty in modern times, nevertheless, these men are guilty of treason and mutiny, and the punishment for both is death. However, in the case of young Ellison, we have cause to complain. Ellison is an extremely young man — he did not "participate" in the mutiny; he suffered severely and unjustly under the unreasonable rule of Captain Bligh and, therefore, it is easy to understand why he would taunt the captain in a moment of crisis. To put a young man to death for a spontaneous second of taunting is tantamount to supreme injustice. Byam complains of this very injustice; he wishes that Ellison were on the train with him to London. He ponders the cruel, infallible nature of sea law. The implacability of this law will be one of the factors that will make Byam consider rejecting civilization and returning to Tahiti. To become a part of this unjust law is difficult for him, and yet he will finally choose the sea as his vocation.

- **a midshipman's dirk** his dagger.

- **the sun had passed the meridian** it had passed the noonday position.

- **epaulettes** ornamental shoulder pieces worn on uniforms.

- **palliating circumstances** attempts to conceal the gravity of a situation.

- **a light chaise** an open carriage, usually with a hood, drawn by a horse.

- **you stand acquitted** you are found innocent of all charges.

- **postscript**   a "P.S." at the bottom of a letter.

- **shanks' mare**   to walk somewhere, rather than ride.

- **carriage and pair**   a carriage and a pair of horses.

CHAPTERS 26 & 27

Summary

Byam goes to see Sir Joseph, who is in the company of Captain Montague, and he informs the two men that he intends to return to the South Sea and to the island of Tahiti. Sir Joseph urges Byam not to return to Tahiti, and Captain Montague tells him that he wants him to sail with him on the *Hector's* next voyage. Byam promises to think the matter over. Sir Joseph then asks Byam if he knows where Christian sailed to after the mutiny, and Byam assures him that he has no idea where Christian was headed, except that Christian's final destination point was an uninhabited island.

Byam reluctantly decides that it is time to return to his family home, Withycombe, and so he hires a coach for the journey. While residing at Withycombe, Byam realizes that his roots are in England – not in Tahiti. He informs Captain Montague and Sir Joseph that he is willing to sail with the captain aboard the *Hector*.

Byam then recounts the events that happened after joining Captain Montague, when the *Hector* was sent to battle against the Dutch. Later, Byam was made captain of a small frigate and received orders to set sail for the South Sea. He recounts the fate of Captain Bligh, how Bligh was made governor of New South Wales, and how some men on the island mutinied against him.

Byam and his small frigate sailed to the South Sea and made a stop at New South Wales, where Byam went ashore to talk to the current leader of the island, one of the island mutineers. Bligh was being held under house arrest until a ship from England sailed to the island to return Bligh to England for a trial of misconduct.

From New South Wales, Byam sailed to Tahiti, where he went ashore and learned that Hitihiti, as well as Byam's wife, Tehani, had died. An old man on the island took Byam to see his daughter, Helen, now grown. Byam met the woman but refrained from telling her that he was her father. The novel closes with Byam contemplating the events of his life and the beauty of Tahiti before returning to his ship.

Commentary

The last two chapters of the novel present the conflict in Byam's soul between his strong desire to return to Tahiti and his friends' argument that he must stay in England and restore the Byam name to its former honor. Even Sir Joseph understands Byam's reluctance to return to the sea; after all, he was in irons in a smelly "hell hole," imprisoned for a long period of time, tried for mutiny and sentenced to death, all unjustly – all because of "sea law" – reason enough for any man to reject having anything to do with naval officers again. However, such people as Captain Montague, who represents the very best that the British navy can offer, stands as a shining example to Byam that more humane people are needed to serve England if she is to become the great colonial power that she seems destined to be. Stereotypes such as Captain Bligh and Captain Edwards should be replaced by men such as Captain Montague.

Not until Byam returns to his home soil, however, does he realize that his roots, like those of his ancestors, are deeply embedded in the values of Western Civilization – in England, in particular – and not in the South Sea.

The Epilogue, as the title indicates, adds nothing to the novel; it simply concludes the story. We hear interesting accounts, such as the West Indies mutiny against Captain Bligh, accusing him of a tyrannical misuse of power, and we also learn that Byam returns to Tahiti, that Tehani is dead, their daughter grown, and that the island has been plagued by missionaries, war, and disease – all of which have destroyed four-fifths of the population. The novel ends with Byam gazing at his granddaughter before departing forever from Tahiti.

- **saving yourself** besides yourself.
- **the portico** a columned porch.
- **men at the sweeps** men at the large oars.
- **chirrup** to make a series of chirps or trilling sounds.
- **the antipodean** on the opposite side of the world.

- **the sinnet**   a braided cordage made in a flat or round or square form from 3 to 9 cords.

CRITICAL ESSAYS

MUTINY ON THE BOUNTY:
THE HISTORICAL BACKGROUND

The Nordhoff and Hall novel is based on an actual, historical mutiny. The authors had at their disposal all of the historical documents associated with this famous mutiny, sometimes called the most celebrated mutiny in the history of navigation. This is due partly to the fact that the mutiny was followed by Captain Bligh's unbelievable South Sea voyage in an open boat, when he navigated over 3,600 miles without the benefit of instruments to bring himself and his loyal adherents to the island of Timor in the East Indies. This extraordinary feat made him a national public hero, and the subsequent capture and trial of some of the men further publicized the incident.

The reason for the *Bounty's* journey is historically the same as in the novel. In 1787, Bligh was appointed captain of the *Bounty*—a rather small, squat ship by the standards of the day—to travel to the island of Tahiti, which Bligh had visited before as an officer under the command of the famous Captain James Cook. The purpose of this trip was to secure breadfruit trees to be transplanted in the West Indies, where the trees would produce cheap food for the slaves owned by the English gentry.

After collecting the breadfruit trees in Tahiti, a task which required several months, during which many of the men became accustomed to the gentle treatment they received from the Tahitian women, the *Bounty* began its homeward journey. One month after leaving Tahiti, the mutiny occurred; Fletcher Christian, Bligh's second-in-command, joined by most of the crew, seized the ship and put Bligh and most of his loyal adherents out to sea in a small boat.

The cause of this mutiny has been a puzzle to everyone who has studied the case. Apparently, Bligh was not much stricter a disciplinarian than the typical captain of that era. The fact that Nordhoff and Hall, as well as the various movies which have been based on the incident, make him an unmitigated villain is not completely borne out by historical evidence. Bligh was clearly an enigmatic man – a victim of three mutinies – yet he was nevertheless promoted in rank after each mutiny, and upon retirement, he achieved the highest rank possible, that of admiral.

THE HISTORICAL WILLIAM BLIGH

Bligh was born in Plymouth, England, in 1754. He went to sea, as did some of the young men on the *Bounty*, when he was only sixteen. His quick mastery of navigation led to his being appointed master on Captain James Cook's ship, the *Resolution*, during Cook's last expedition to the Tahitian Islands. After this trip, Bligh was involved in the English wars and was appointed master of a frigate and participated and distinguished himself in several battles. By the end of the war, he had earned the rank of lieutenant and was appointed captain of the *Bounty* when he was only thirty-two years old.

After Bligh's incredible voyage over the open seas, he reached England, and the mutiny became such an important issue that the government sent Captain Edward Edwards in the *Pandora* to search out, find, and return the mutineers for trial. By the time Edwards reached Tahiti, Fletcher Christian and eight others had left in the *Bounty* and had settled on an uncharted island named Pitcairn, where they lived undisturbed until 1808, and where their descendants still live. Of those found in Tahiti, three were found guilty and were hanged.

Meanwhile, Bligh's career continued to prosper. He returned again to Tahiti, and, this time, successfully fulfilled his mission of transplanting the breadfruit trees to the West Indies. In 1797, while captain of another ship (the *Director*), his crew mutinied, and, this time, Bligh was simply put ashore and left behind. In 1805, he was made governor of New South Wales, Australia, and after three years, his subjects revolted (mutinied) against him and sent him under arrest back to England because of his "oppressive behavior." Back in England, however, the "mutineers" were found guilty of conspiracy, and Bligh was again promoted – first, to rear admiral and, later, to vice admiral. Bligh died in London in 1817.

Before Bligh died, however, because of the extreme publicity of the *Bounty* mutiny and the subsequent trials, Bligh published a short report of the mutiny. It sold so well that, with the help of an editor, he expanded the work into a full-length account of the entire voyage. His account, however, has one major flaw: its omissions. Many significant facts are simply not alluded to. He mentions, for example, that even though the crew was an inefficient and worthless lot, he never noticed any signs of discontent among them. Furthermore, he offers an explanation for the short rations: he anticipated that the voyage might take much longer than previously thought, so meals were meager. His explanation of why Fletcher Christian overtook the ship is considered by many critics to be quite valid; elsewhere, Bligh reports that Christian was of such a passionate nature that he was subject to "outbursts of perspiration, especially in his hands so that he soiled whatever he touched," and that he was inordinately fond of women.

Bligh's character has been variously interpreted. He has been described as a brutal, oppressive tyrant who cheated his crew of their rightful rations and withheld their pay. Yet others have praised Bligh as a master navigator (even his detractors concede this), who contributed significantly to the charting of the South Sea and was a brave naval officer who conducted himself heroically in many sea battles. He does not seem to have been unduly tyrannical; it was common to flog seamen who showed any signs of disrespect to their officers, but all accounts agree that Bligh had an abusive tongue, which he used against his officers in front of common seamen. This practice was highly unethical. Bligh's overzealous and overbearing manner made him a very unpopular commander, as witnessed by the subsequent mutinies against him. Professionally, however, he was above reproach.

MOVIES BASED ON THE MUTINY ON THE *BOUNTY*

Some books or novels lend themselves to movie adaptation. Often, these books are romantic or adventure stories, such as *The Three Musketeers* or *Mutiny on the Bounty*. Since the historical mutiny aboard the *Bounty* in 1789, there have been three highly successful books about the incident: (1) Captain William Bligh's *The Mutiny on Board H.M.S. Bounty*, (2) Nordhoff and Hall's *Mutiny on the Bounty*, and (3) Robert Hough's *The Bounty*. Likewise, there have been three highly successful movies based on the incident: *Mutiny on the Bounty* (1935), starring Clark Gable and Charles Laughton; *Mutiny on the Bounty* (1962), starring Marlon Brando and Trevor Howard; and *The Bounty*

(1984), starring Mel Gibson and Anthony Hopkins. Each movie follows its source book to some extent; likewise, each movie digresses from its source book in some instances. All of the movies, however, have one thing in common: they give a much more important role to Fletcher Christian than do any of the books; not surprisingly, each movie features a popular matinee idol of the time.

Of the major movies, the first one follows the Nordhoff and Hall novel the most closely, especially in the latter sections of the novel. The most recently released movie, *The Bounty*, follows the general plot, yet differs greatly in that the narration is told from Bligh's point of view. The 1962 version focuses on the adventure of the trip to Tahiti – the trials and tribulations of getting there, and the arrival at these idyllic islands. After the mutiny, the men discover Pitcairn Island, where Christian is accidentally killed because of the indiscretion of the mutineers.

A key difference between the movies and the books on which the mutiny is based lies in the motivations for the mutiny itself. The books are more complex and somewhat more believable for most readers; for others, the films are more believable in that the reasons for the mutiny are graphically presented: (1) the captain, maniacal in his pursuit of a short cut to the West Indies, would have carried his men and his ship to an almost certain death and (2) the men wish to return to their women in Tahiti and to their idyllic existence there.

Mutiny on the Bounty (1935), starring Clark Gable, Hollywood's all-time favorite matinee idol, and Charles Laughton.

This movie is closely based on the Nordhoff and Hall novel; however, one should be aware of the differences between the novel and the movie. First, in the movie, the sailors are "impressed," or forced, into service aboard the *Bounty* and thus have no feeling of allegiance to Bligh. In the novel, the sailors actively petition the captain of the ship for the honor of service aboard the *Bounty*. Therefore, the mutiny in the movie is *not* carried out by loyal British seamen who are respected members of the navy, but, instead, by the scum of the bars and jails, men who have no interest in anything but themselves. Perhaps the director erred; the mutiny is a much more grave and serious affair when it is committed by loyal seamen than when committed by low-class riff-raff.

Another difference concerns Tinkler; in the book, he is punished by being placed in the topmast until he is almost frozen; in the movie, this punishment is meted out to Byam. Since the focus of a two-hour movie cannot develop many of the various individuals who are in a long novel, it must logically center its episodes on key characters.

In the novel, the antagonism between Bligh and Christian is gradually developed. In contrast, in the movie, Christian and Bligh are set up immediately as polar opposites. From the very first scene, Christian sees himself as a defender of the underdog and defies Captain Bligh's unreasonable demands. True, Christian is the man who "kidnapped" the men from the saloons, but he was simply following orders from the tyrannical Captain Bligh.

The movie presents Bligh as a villain from the very first scene. It does not show him as having a single redeeming quality. He is a satanic creature, bound to have his way; he delights in imposing suffering on the common seamen, as well as on his ranking officers. Bligh is sadistic in his punishment and totally authoritarian in his absolute rule. The audience dislikes him immensely – partly due to Charles Laughton's superbly villainous performance.

This is the only movie to include scenes showing the return to England and the trial of Byam, even though the role is capsulated, compared to the novel. Some fifty years after its making, this early *Bounty* movie is still a powerful motion picture.

Mutiny on the Bounty (1962), starring two-time Academy Award winner Marlon Brando, Trevor Howard, and Richard Harris as "Mills."

This version of the story of the *Bounty* differs from the Nordhoff and Hall novel and also from the other movie adaptations in that the plight of Fletcher Christian, once he leaves the prisoners on Tahiti, after seizing the ship and setting Bligh adrift, is presented in its entirety. While and Nordhoff and Hall's *Mutiny* doesn't follow Christian's escapades once he leaves Tahiti in search of an uninhabited island, this movie does. Christian anchors at Pitcairn Island, an island in the South Sea, positioned incorrectly on the official British sea charts.

The major emphasis in the movie is on the different social classes which Bligh and Christian come from. Bligh, a low-brow who understands nothing of the gentry, feels that all upper-class people are spineless and ineffectual; he is characterized as a complete opposite of Christian, who, as the penultimate gentleman, respects the laws of the king, but will not let any man debase his character. Indeed, the strong contrast between the two men's characters is an added catalyst to all of the climactic events in the movie – from the squabbling the two men do while journeying to Tahiti to the actual act of mutiny itself.

Here, the motivation for the mutiny is manifold, including the meager half-ration of water which the men are allowed while taking the breadfruit trees to the West Indies, the sadistic punishment Bligh hands out, and the apparent enjoyment he gains from it. Three men are killed in this *Bounty* movie, whereas in the novel, not one man perishes in the journey before the mutiny occurs, and the explosive incident which finally sparks the mutiny occurs when Bligh kicks a ladle from Christian's hand while Christian, disobeying a direct command of Bligh's, attempts to give fresh water in the name of humanity to a man delirious after drinking salt water. This scene does not occur in the novel.

Here, we clearly see the distinction between Bligh's and Christian's social backgrounds. After Bligh has kicked the ladle out of Christian's hand, Christian immediately knocks Bligh to the deck in outrage. Bligh orders Fryer to imprison Christian for striking a superior officer, and it is at that moment when Christian gathers arms and seizes the ship. It should be noted that Mills, who has a much larger role in the movie than in the novel or in the other two movies, has been goading Christian to seize the ship ever since the *Bounty* set sail from Tahiti.

This *Bounty* movie covers much more fully the events of Christian's flight after the mutiny than do the other two movies and the books, and, in doing so, it presents a deeper understanding of the motives behind Christian's actions. It is Christian's gentlemanly intention from the first moments after the mutiny to return to England and be tried for mutiny in order to bring public attention to the sadistic and ruthless conditions that captains such as Bligh submit their men to. Hopefully, his testimony will rid the world of such tyrants forever. However, when Christian reveals his plan to Mills and the other mutineers on Pitcairn Island, the men are alarmed. Their deaths are virtually assured if they return to England. That night, Mills and some of the other mutineers burn the *Bounty*, and Christian, trying to save his sexton from raging flames, is badly burned from a falling mast. His followers pull him from the ship and try to resuscitate him, but their efforts fail, and Christian dies on the beach.

The Bounty (1984), starring Mel Gibson and Anthony Hopkins.

Director Roger Donaldson's *The Bounty* is adapted from Richard Hough's novel, and it differs from the novel and from other adaptations in that the story-line is told to the viewer by Bligh himself (Bligh is a lieutenant in the movie and hopes to become a captain after he successfully delivers the breadfruit trees). One serious flaw in Bligh's narration is that he could never have known what became of the *Bounty* or the events which took place on the *Bounty* after he was set adrift, yet the *Bounty*'s plight after the mutineers set Bligh adrift is examined closely in this movie.

The difference in point-of-view is a major factor when comparing this movie to the two earlier ones. The scene of Bligh's being court-martialed by Admiral Hood and the tribunal begins the movie, and it is Bligh's flashbacks which constitute the "meat" of the movie. Bligh is being tried for conduct unbecoming an officer; the emphasis is not on how or why the mutineers took the *Bounty*, but, rather, on why Bligh lost the ship. For the modern audience, this is more believable than the original plot-line.

Another difference in this movie, when compared with other works associated with the incident, is the personal relationship between Bligh and Christian. Cordial yet stiff in the original novel and in the other, earlier movies, a friendship exists here between the two men before the *Bounty* sets sail and it lasts throughout the ship's journey to Tahiti. It is not until after the *Bounty* reaches Tahiti and Christian is allowed to go ashore that the relationship between the two men becomes strained. Bligh is intensely jealous of Christian — particularly of Christian's relationship with the Tahitian women. Subtle overtones of Bligh's latent homosexuality exist in Hough's novel and are incorporated into the movie which was adapted from the book. Early in both works, the two men are on a first-name basis with each other, but once Bligh becomes jealous of Christian's sexual behavior on the island, proper names and ranks are used henceforth in bitter, sarcastic tones.

In this particular movie, Lieutenant Bligh is seen in a much more sympathetic light than in the earlier adaptations from books. This is brought about by a number of factors, including the narrative's being told from Bligh's perspective, the absence of overt and useless violence in the journey before reaching Tahiti (the only instance of violence occuring when two men are gagged by Master Fryer's orders, and it is Bligh himself who gives Christian the order to untie the two men), the heroic struggle to reach England in a small launch, which Bligh and his followers are allowed to use (Bligh gives up his food so that others who are delirious may have a better chance to survive), and the final scene of the movie, which focuses on the emotional Bligh, exonerated of all crimes charged against him, weeping before the tribunal.

The motivation behind Christian's seizing of the *Bounty* is more plausible in this novel than in many of the other associated works. It is after Bligh informs the crew and the officers that he is planning to circumnavigate the globe by going around the Cape of Good Hope, just as he unsuccessfully attempted during the journey to Tahiti, that Christian and his followers seize the ship. Also, the bond that many of the men aboard the *Bounty* form with women on Tahiti (Christian falls in love the daughter of the island chief and she becomes pregnant) are critical factors in the decision to seize the ship. The conditions on board the *Bounty* and the treatment of the men by Bligh are only minor reasons for the men to seize the ship, but, coupled with Bligh's plan to sail around the Cape of Good Hope and the yearning of the men to return to Tahiti, mutiny seems inevitable.

SUGGESTED ESSAY QUESTIONS

(1) Discuss the novel in terms of its being a novel of adventure.

(2) Discuss the influence which Tahiti and its inhabitants have upon the crew of the *Bounty* and the importance of this influence as a factor leading up to the mutiny.

(3) Discuss the varying factors which lead the men to mutiny against Captain Bligh. Consider the question of why these factors are not offered as mitigating circumstances during the court-martial.

(4) Discuss the relevancy of "sea law" and the need for such a stringent law.

(5) If you have seen one of the movies, discuss the relationship between Bligh and Christian in the Nordhoff and Hall novel and contrast and compare it to the relationship between the two men in the film.

(6) Discuss the effect of restricted rationing and unreasonable punishment on the seamen.

(7) Discuss the effect of Bligh's constant accusations of stealing on the men's morale.

(8) Discuss the court-martial in terms of modern jurisprudence.

(9) Discuss the authors' "resurrecting" Tinkler to bring about the resolution of the novel and Byam's innocence.

(10) After the indignities suffered by Byam at the hands of unjust naval officers, discuss the factors which motivate Byam to return to life in the navy rather than to Tahiti.

SELECTED BIBLIOGRAPHY

BLIGH, WILLIAM. *The Mutiny on Board H.M.S. Bounty.* Signet Classic, 1961. The "Afterword" by Milton Rugoff is well worth reading.

BRIAND, JR., PAUL L. *In Search of Paradise: The Nordhoff-Hall Story.* New York: Duell, Sloan & Peace, 1966.

MACKANESS, GEORGE. *The Life of Vice-Admiral William Bligh.* 2 vols. London: Angus and Robertson, 1931. New York, Farrar & Rinehart, Inc., 1936.

MONTGOMERIE, H. S. *William Bligh of the Bounty in Fact and in Fable.* London: Williams and Norgate, Ltd., 1937.

RAWSON, GEOFFREY. *Bligh of the Bounty.* New York: G. R. Gorman, 1937.

RUTTER, OWEN. *Turbulent Journey: A Life of William Bligh, Vice-Admiral of the Blue.* London: Ivor Nicholson & Watson, Ltd., 1936.

NOTES

NOTES

NOTES

NOTES

NOTES

NOTES